# DE HAVILLAND COMET
## The World's First Commercial Jetliner

# DE HAVILLAND COMET

## The World's First Commercial Jetliner

COLIN HIGGS

AIR WORLD

**AIR WORLD**

## De Havilland Comet
## The World's First Commercial Jetliner

First published in Great Britain in 2018 by
Air World Books
An imprint of
Pen & Sword Books Ltd
Yorkshire - Philadelphia

ISBN 978 1 52671 961 4

A CIP catalogue record for this book is
available from the British Library

Typeset in 10/12 pt Palatino
by Aura Technology and Software Services, India

Printed and bound by Replika Press Pvt. Ltd.

Pen & Sword Books Ltd incorporates the Imprints of Aviation, Atlas,
Family History, Fiction, Maritime, Military, Discovery, Politics, History,
Archaeology, Select, Wharncliffe Local History, Wharncliffe True Crime,
Military Classics, Wharncliffe Transport, Leo Cooper, The Praetorian Press,
Remember When, Seaforth Publishing and Frontline Publishing.

For a complete list of Pen & Sword titles please contact

PEN & SWORD BOOKS LTD
47 Church Street, Barnsley, South Yorkshire, S70 2AS, England
E-mail: enquiries@pen-and-sword.co.uk
Website: www.pen-and-sword.co.uk

Or

PEN AND SWORD BOOKS
1950 Lawrence Rd, Havertown, PA 19083, USA
E-mail: Uspen-and-sword@casematepublishers.com
Website: www.penandswordbooks.com

# Contents

# Acknowledgement

The author would like to thank Barry Guess and Trevor Friend at BAE Systems Heritage for their kind and unfailing assistance in supplying images for this book.

# Introduction

THE PRESS WAS not best pleased. Having been invited along to the de Havilland factory at Hatfield to inspect the new, exciting, jet-powered Comet airliner, journalists were instead given a detailed briefing. They were, however, earnestly assured that the first flight would not happen until the inclement weather improved.

An artist's impression of Comet 1 G-ALYP, the first delivered and the first to fly commercially. (BAE SYSTEMS)

Test pilot John Cunningham had made several taxi runs earlier in the day and
even a short hop of about 200 yards. He now impressed the visitors with full power,
ear-splitting jet engine tests before the aircraft was jacked up so an undercarriage
test could be performed, at which time the journalists trooped out of the airfield to
write their stories for the next issues.

At about 5pm that same afternoon, with the checks duly completed, Cunningham made a snap decision to undertake the first flight immediately. Just one hour later, with all four Ghost engines performing perfectly, the Comet prototype took to the skies for the first time.

It was 27 July 1949, barely four years after the Second World War and less than seven years since the formation of a committee that would set Britain's aircraft industry on a path to peacetime development.

Britain had stolen a march on the mighty American aircraft manufacturers and led the world in jet airliner development. If only they could hold onto that advantage.

The prototype Comet taxiing out for its first flight in front of a growing crowd of de Havilland workers. (BAE SYSTEMS)

# CHAPTER 1

# Genesis

THE AVAILABILITY OF money and the concentration of minds on beating the enemy means that wartime always speeds up technical development, and the years of the Second World War were no different. Britain's prowess at building bombers and fighters was second to none, though the United States had similarly progressed with its work on both military and civil transport aircraft with the ubiquitous Douglas C-47 leading the way.

United Airlines' Douglas DC-3 NC16070 with passengers waiting for their flight from New York to Los Angeles in 1937. The DC-3 was the apotheosis of pre-war airliner design. (John Stroud Collection at AFH)

It became obvious that when the war ended Britain would have to either send back, pay for or destroy all the aircraft that had come from the USA under the terms of the lend-lease agreement. The UK would need to buy new American transports for civil requirements, while the USA would have no need for any British military aircraft.

At the same time, Britain's vital aircraft industry would founder without new orders to replace the deluge of work received during the war. So at a time when it was assumed that all of the government's concentration would be on winning the war, they formed a committee with the sole aim of winning the peace – or, to put it accurately, to decide how best to tackle the requirements of civil aviation in Britain, its Empire and the Commonwealth after the fighting had ended.

John Moore-Brabazon was an aristocratic car enthusiast who became one of Britain's earliest aviation pioneers. He had flown for the first time in France, taking to the air in a Voisin biplane in November 1908. In 1910, at the age of 26, Moore-Brabazon became the holder of British pilot license No.1 and on the same day one of his best friends, Charles Rolls of Rolls-Royce fame, was awarded license No.2. Unlike Rolls, however, Moore-Brabazon survived his early months of flying and became one of the most important people in British aviation and the Comet story.

After serving with the Royal Flying Corps in the First World War, Brabazon stood for Parliament in 1918, becoming the Conservative MP for Chatham. Having worked his way through the party until he was made Minister of Transport in 1940, Brabazon took on the vital role of Minister of Aircraft Production in 1942.

John Moore-Brabazon doing what he loved before flying took over, taking part in the French Grand Prix at Dieppe in 1908. (Private Collection)

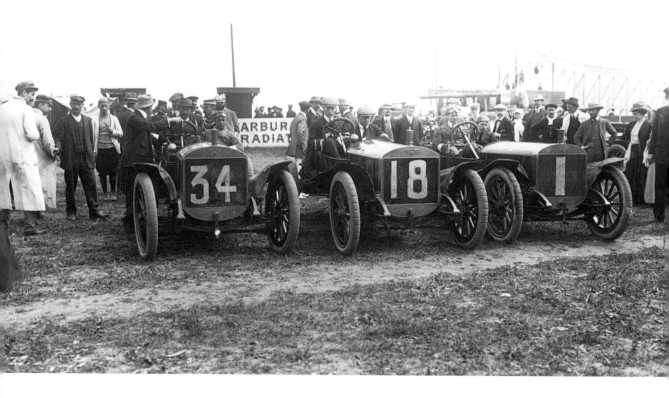

Unfortunately some uncompromising opinions forced his resignation at which point he was elevated to the House of Lords with the title of Lord Brabazon of Tara.

With his background Brabazon was ideally placed to chair the new committee. The initial report came out quickly, within just a few months, and recommended a variety of aircraft to fulfill different roles. It was decided that the work demanded a second committee, again named after its chairman, to develop plans further and advise the government on how best to implement the first committee's recommendations. This new committee included representatives from the Ministry of Aircraft Production, the Air Ministry and BOAC. The sole representative from an aircraft manufacturer was Geoffrey de Havilland.

It was initially proposed that six new aircraft types would be needed to fulfill all requirements. The committee released updates at various stages, each time providing further information about one of the types, until it presented its final report in 1945. By this time, the committee had already asked for tenders for its planned aircraft, and, in some cases, contracts had been issued. What emerged was virtually every civil aircraft design, successful or otherwise, built in Britain over the next ten years.

The contract for a Type I high-quality trans-Atlantic airliner was awarded to Bristol Aircraft. The massive Brabazon eight radial-engine airliner was destined to fly around 100 passengers across the Atlantic in luxury but never created the interest with airlines that had been expected. The single example flew in 1949, only to end up being scrapped in 1953.

Lord Brabazon photographed in March 1951.

The Bristol Brabazon, a massive eight-engine airliner named after the committee chairman. However, it was too big and expensive for the new post-war world of commercial aviation. (John Stroud Collection at AFH)

The Type II contract was more complicated. It was originally supposed to be for a feederliner, an aircraft to replace the pre-war Dragon Rapide and the DC-3. However BEA, destined to be the prime user, wanted something bigger. The revised decision was to split the new aircraft into two separate contracts.

Airspeed, the company co-founded by bestselling novelist and aircraft engineer Nevil Shute, delivered the Type IIa, which became the Ambassador. Vickers, for its part, received the Type IIb contract. This became the Vickers Viscount, the world's first turboprop airliner, of which 445 were built and which became one of the most successful aircraft to come from the considerations of the Brabazon Committee.

The Type III contract for a large medium-range airliner designed to fly the Empire routes was also given to Bristol Aircraft. The Britannia turboprop was more successful than the Brabazon, with a total of eighty-five being built. However problems with icing caused delays to its engine development and this meant that it went into service just a year before the Boeing 707, restricting the potential customer base.

Dan-Air's Airspeed Ambassador G-AMAE at Gatwick in 1961. (Peter Keating Collection at AFH)

Contracts for the final two aircraft went to de Havilland which was based at Hatfield in Hertfordshire. This was the company that had perhaps been Britain's most successful aircraft manufacturer between the wars, with its range of Moths and the graceful Dragon Rapide among many others. The Mosquito had kept the production line at full capacity during the Second World War but the company knew it would slow and it was vital that the factories had more to do.

Vickers Viscount G-AOHW of British Airways at Wick in the far north of Scotland in 1975. (AFH)

BOAC's Bristol Britannia G-ANBE in flight. (AFH)

A new Type V was added by the committee which revived the original small feederliner concept. This was the de Havilland Dove which first flew as early as 1945 and which sold in large numbers to airlines and air forces around the world. Other similar variants were then built, such as the Devon and the Sea Devon for Britain's armed forces, and the Heron, which was a stretched four-engine version.

By far the most radical aircraft to come from the committee was the Type IV, a fully jet-powered airliner, the de Havilland Comet. Geoffrey de Havilland had urged the committee to support the concept, one that perhaps only his company had the experience to create. De Havilland had done much pioneering work in jet-powered designs for the RAF, aircraft such as the Vampire fighter, and was developing jet engines in-house as well. De Havilland was duly awarded the contract; now they had to make it work.

Frank, later Sir Frank, Whittle is credited with designing the first jet engine in the 1930s and in a few short years the idea came to fruition when he ran his Power Jets WU for the first time in April 1937. Official indifference to the concept caused financial difficulties for Power Jets until 1939 when the Air Ministry finally understood the value and potential of the jet engine and provided funds for the business.

De Havilland's successful short haul airliner, the Dove. Here is an RAF example used for transport and communications flights. (AFH)

The Comet 1 prototype on one of its many test flights in August 1949. (BAE SYSTEMS)

The Gloster E28/39, powered by a Whittle jet engine, flew for the first time in May 1941, though the first press release announcing the extent of British secret jet engine projects was not published until January 1944. By then there were more than ten jet projects in development from almost every engine manufacturer in Britain. Rolls-Royce had three, and there were others from Metropolitan Vickers (Metrovick), Armstrong Siddeley and Bristol.

There was another aircraft engineer, Frank Halford, who was already hard at work in his London design consultancy on a simplified version of the Whittle engine. The Halford H-1 flew in both the Gloster Meteor and de Havilland Vampire in 1943, at which time Halford's company was bought by de Havilland. Halford was employed to run the newly-formed de Havilland Engine Company, the H-1 was renamed as the Goblin, and work continued on an uprated engine, the Ghost.

So all the building blocks were in place when de Havilland was given authority to go ahead with its jet-powered airliner in 1945. The company now built airframes and engines. It had vast experience of building aircraft both for civil airlines and for the military as well as, importantly, a design and manufacturing team second to none. Helpfully, within a few months the company would also have access to captured data from German aircraft designers. The DH106 was ready to go.

Sir Frank Whittle in the uniform of a Group Captain in the RAF. (John Stroud Collection at AFH)

Britain's first jet-powered aircraft, the Gloster E28/39 W4041-G, which flew in May 1941. (BAE SYSTEMS)

A Vampire F.1, TG278 which was fitted with a Ghost engine, in flight. (John Stroud Collection at AFH)

# FRANK HALFORD

In the years before the First World War you were likely to find the young Frank Halford at Brooklands near Weybridge in Surrey. That said, he was not working on an early wood, wire and canvas aircraft, rather as a speedy young driver on the banked racing circuit.

Halford, however, could not stay away from aviation for long and in 1913, at the age of 19, he took his first flying lesson at Brooklands and soon became a flying instructor. It was as an engineer though that he started working in the business. He inspected engines for the Air Ministry then joined the Royal Flying Corps during the war. Later, as Major Halford, he joined engine manufacturer Ricardos and worked on motorbike engines for the next few years until he set up his own engineering consultancy in 1923.

One of his first customers was his old friend Geoffrey de Havilland who was looking for an engine for his new light aircraft, the Moth. Halford's Cirrus engine was followed by the hugely successful Gipsy series which became the engine of choice for thousands of inter-war light aircraft.

For the next few years Halford's expertise was in great demand not only from de Havilland but also Vickers and Napier. For Napier he designed the Sabre engine which was developed

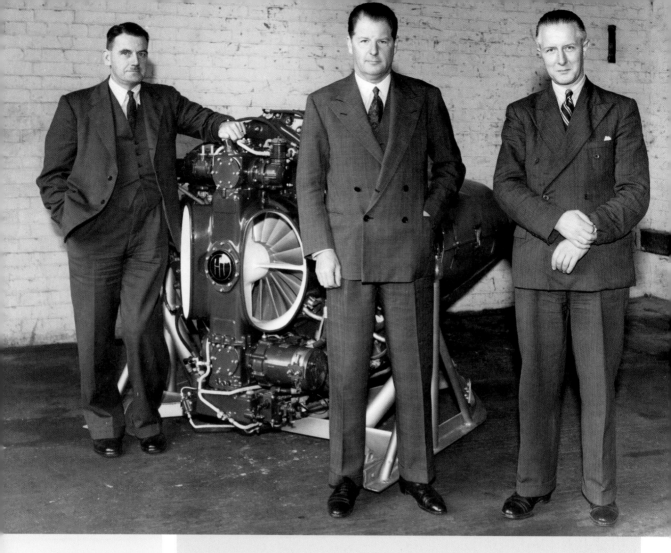

Frank Halford (centre) with long term associates John Brodie (left) and Dr. ES Moult (right) pictured at de Havilland in 1945. (BAE SYSTEMS)

into one of the world's most powerful piston aero engines and which was fitted in the Tempest and Typhoon.

During the Second World War Halford worked closely with de Havilland, initially on propellers, but from 1941 on jet engine development. His design was a simplified version of the Whittle and went on to become the Goblin and the Ghost, powering all of de Havilland's early jet aircraft. As mentioned, in 1944 his business was bought out and he became technical director of the newly-formed de Havilland Engine Company, becoming a main board director of de Havilland the following year.

Halford was made a CBE in 1948. He passed away at the early age of 61 in 1955.

# CHAPTER 2

# Building the Comet

THE INITIAL SPECIFICATION for de Havilland's radical jet-powered airliner, the Comet, was that it should be a trans-Atlantic mail-carrier able to fly at 400mph (644kph), at 40,000 ft (12,192m) and carry twenty-four passengers non-stop across the Atlantic. The secret of the proposed airliner would always be the ability to juggle the huge potential of the jet engine against the needs of the airlines.

It needed to be faster and fly higher. It also needed to be smoother, vibration-free and more economical to run, both in fuel usage and in maintenance.

De Havilland test pilots John Cunningham (left) and John Derry preparing for another display at an air show. (BAE SYSTEMS)

At an early stage captured German data convinced the design team that the new airliner should have swept wings. These meant less drag and less drag meant improved performance. Too much sweep on the wings, however, meant loss of control and the loss of ability to carry a large payload. At one point de Havilland considered a swept wing, tail-less airliner for which they built research aircraft to test the idea.

Three DH108 Swallows were built with a forty-three degree sweep back, and painstaking research flying was undertaken from Hatfield with test pilot John Derry at the controls for most of the flights. The high point was when Derry, perhaps inadvertently, broke the sound barrier on 6 September 1948, becoming the first Briton to do so.

Much interesting and useful data was collected, but all three aircraft were eventually lost in fatal crashes. The first killed Geoffrey de Havilland Jr in September 1946. When de Havilland had completed its work, the remaining two aircraft were handed over to the Royal Aircraft Establishment (RAE) at Farnborough for further research. However, the second crashed in February 1950, killing its RAE pilot, Squadron Leader Stuart Muller-Rowland; the third crashed just a few months later while in the hands of Squadron Leader George Genders.

John Derry flying DH108 Swallow VW120, the third prototype, in February 1948, some months before he became the first Briton to break the sound barrier. (BAE SYSTEMS)

Time was against the designers as the huge US manufacturers were already producing their first post-war airliners, types such as the Constellation, Stratocruiser and Douglas DC-6. If de Havilland was to help win a share of international airline business with a British-built aircraft, the company realised it had no time to iron out the problems of the radical DH108.

The final concept was, therefore, more conventional than originally intended. The wings were designed with a modest twenty degree sweep back and a tail was reintroduced. One major part of the original plan that remained, however, was that the aircraft would be powered by four de Havilland Ghost engines, the up-rated version of Frank Halford's original Goblin.

Practically de Havilland was also able to guarantee performance requirements for their main client, BOAC, despite a requested increase in passenger numbers from twenty-four to thirty-six.

By January 1947 there were orders for sixteen aircraft on de Havilland's books. Two were for the Ministry of Supply, BOAC had ordered eight and British South American Airways a further six, although after it was announced that BSAA would be merged with BOAC this order was cancelled and BOAC increased its original order to nine.

Having settled on a final configuration the hard work began. Flight controls, undercarriage, fuel tanks and even the method of attaching metal to metal were new.

De Havilland's famous Mosquito had been made of wood and bonded with glue so there was plenty of experience working with adhesives. In 1936 de Havilland had invested money in resin-based glue research and one of the outcomes was Redux cement. First used on the Dove in 1945 Redux was now employed using heat and pressure in both the wing and fuselage to provide a lighter and smoother way of joining metal to metal. Less rivets again meant less drag and less weight and every ounce saved put money back in their clients' pockets. The use of Redux in the

The Comet's new engine, the de Havilland Ghost. (BAE SYSTEMS)

Comet 1 G-ALYP was the first production jet airliner, here under construction in June 1950. (BAE SYSTEMS)

production of the wing had another very important purpose. The vast amount of fuel to be carried, up to 40% of the maximum weight, meant that the fuel tanks in the wings had to be integral rather than separate structures. Rivets meant holes and holes could easily mean leaks so a rivet-less fuel tank was both safer and more economical.

The aircraft's nose was specially designed, again to reduce drag. A DH106 nose was flown on a wartime Horsa glider fuselage to make sure that rainfall cleared easily from the windscreen.

A mock-up of the Comet nose attached to Horsa glider TL348 on 19 December 1946. (BAE SYSTEMS)

Nothing was left to chance as most aspects were new and everything had to be tested to destruction, amended and tested again. A massive new decompression chamber was built at Hatfield where fuselage sections were exposed to conditions found at up to 70,000 ft (21,336m) and temperatures as low as minus 70 degrees C (minus 94 degrees F).

The new engines were flown for the first time on 24 July 1947 when two Merlins on an Avro Lancastrian were replaced with Ghosts. These were but a few of the thousands of processes that had to be refined or reinvented to deal with a radical concept such as this jet airliner.

By the spring of 1949 the new airliner was in the final stages of production. It had been given the name Comet only in December 1948, but little information had been made available and it seems that most of the press were happy for this brave new British concept to stay secretive and away from prying foreign eyes.

On Saturday 2 April 1949 the completed Comet prototype, G-5-1 but later to be re-registered as G-ALVG, was pushed gently out of its hangar at Hatfield so that engine testing could begin. The two starboard engines were still to be fitted but the shape of the aircraft could be seen and the scream of jet engines on a commercial aircraft could be heard for the first time.

Avro Lancastrian VM703, seen here in August 1947, was used to test the de Havilland Ghost engines after the outer Merlins had been removed. (Private Collection)

The Comet 1 prototype under construction in the hangar at Hatfield in 1949. (BAE SYSTEMS)

The new Comet 1 prototype in the open air for ground testing on 2 April 1949. (BAE SYSTEMS)

Just two days before the first flight, the Comet 1 prototype emerges from the hangar at Hatfield to begin its first taxi runs. (BAE SYSTEMS)

Confidence was high at de Havilland. Not only had the company completed the prototype from authorisation to production in barely four years, but it had sixteen airframes in the factory in various stages of completion.

By July the early testing was completed. On 25 July the Comet began taxi runs along the Hatfield runway followed by a day of 'snagging' before she emerged again on 27 July. More taxi runs were followed by a series of 'short hops' before the press and gathered onlookers were allowed to inspect the aircraft. At about 4.30pm the chief inspector was satisfied with the aircraft and chief test pilot, John Cunningham, made a decision to take the momentous first flight immediately.

De Havilland staff began to emerge from the factory and offices as word went round that their aircraft was about to fly. Soon after 6pm Cunningham released the brakes, thundered down the runway and took off. The flight lasted thirty-one minutes during which time the Comet reached 10,000 ft (3,048m).

Handling qualities were tested at various speeds before Cunningham landed. He promptly reported that everything had performed well. The age of the commercial jet airliner had begun.

The Comet prototype outside for engine tests the day before the first flight. (BAE SYSTEMS)

The Comet 1 prototype on one of its 'short hops' on 27 July 1949. (BAE SYSTEMS)

A shot of the Comet 1 prototype on its first flight on 27 July 1949. (BAE SYSTEMS)

The Comet 1 prototype airborne on 27 July 1949. (BAE SYSTEMS)

The Comet prototype is surrounded by de Havilland staff after the first flight. (BAE SYSTEMS)

# THE DE HAVILLAND COMET TEAM

By sheer coincidence the first flight of the Comet took place not only on Geoffrey de Havilland's 67th birthday, but on John Cunningham's 32nd. Both men were just part of the remarkable team that had brought the Comet from the vaguest of initial ideas to flight.

De Havilland himself was born in Buckinghamshire and went to school at St Edward's Oxford, the establishment that would later educate RAF legends such as Douglas Bader, Guy Gibson and Adrian Warburton. He studied engineering and worked in the motor car industry before borrowing money to build an aircraft which promptly crashed the first time he tried to fly it.

De Havilland sold his second aircraft to His Majesty's Balloon Factory and eventually was employed by Airco at Hendon as a designer. When motorcycle manufacturer BSA bought Airco and wanted to use the factory for producing cars, de Havilland borrowed enough to buy out the aviation assets and start his own business.

The de Havilland Aircraft Company was formed in 1920 at Stag Lane in Edgware before moving to Hatfield in 1933. In the process one of the world's most famous aviation companies was born, a company that went on to build aircraft, engines and propellers in house.

Over the next thirty-five years, with Geoffrey de Havilland at the helm the company produced a stream of classic, and best-selling, aircraft, both for civil and military use. Paramount among them was the series of Moths, built in their thousands throughout the

1920s and 30s, and airliners such as the Hercules, Flamingo and the ubiquitous Dragon Rapide, before the company turned its hand to creating one of the great wartime aircraft, the Mosquito.

At the same time that Gloster was developing the jet-powered Meteor, de Havilland's Vampire spawned a series of twin-boom air force and navy fighters including the Venom and Sea Vixen.

Since the beginning at Stag Lane de Havilland had surrounded himself with a talented team of designers and engineers. Charles 'CC' Walker, for example, was a founding director and chief engineer who worked with Geoffrey at Airco and stayed alongside him until retirement in 1954.

Chief designer was Ronald Bishop who was responsible for the designs of the Mosquito, Hornet, Vampire and Dove. He had joined de Havilland in 1921 as an apprentice and remained there until 1964. Two other key members were Richard Clarkson, the man who had been responsible for the Mosquito's aerodynamics and now performed the same task with the Comet, and Bill Tamblin, who looked after the wings.

This remarkable team, together with a legion of draughtsmen, engineers and designers, not only produced a remarkable aircraft in a very short time, but had to solve a brand new set of problems. Never before had aircraft engineers had to cope with these levels of compressibility and drag. For the first time they were dealing with enormous volumes of air entering jet intakes. All of these issues are now daily occurrences with the thousands of jet airliners flying today, but then it was new. The Comet was first.

With Frank Halford in control of the engines the team was in need of just one more person, someone to actually fly the aircraft. John Cunningham originally joined de Havilland in 1935, at the age of 18 on a three-year technical training contract, but by 1939

*Sir Geoffrey de Havilland seen here in 1951 (Flight)*

*Probably Sir Geoffrey de Havilland's greatest creation, the Tiger Moth. Here is G-APBI seen at Baginton in 1958. (AFH)*

One of eleven DH66
Hercules airliners
built in the 1920s.
They were operated
by Imperial Airways,
West Australian
Airways and the
South African Air
Force. (John Stroud
Collection at AFH)

The great de
Havilland Mosquito.
This is the RAF's FBVI
NT193 in flight in 1944.
(BAE SYSTEMS)

Some of the key members of the Comet programme. They are Chief engineer Charles 'CC' Walker (top left); Chief designer Ronald Bishop (top right); and left to right in bottom image, CC Walker, Sir Geoffrey de Havilland, Chief aerodynamicist Richard Clarkson, Ronald Bishop. (BAE SYSTEMS)

he was working as a junior test pilot under de Havilland's son, Geoffrey Jr. Called up in August 1939 Cunningham soon became one of the RAF's most successful night fighter pilots, flying a Beaufighter and shooting down a number of German bombers during the winter of 1940-41.

Cunningham had visited Hatfield early in 1941 to take his first look at a Mosquito. As Commanding Officer of the newly Mosquito-equipped 85 Squadron throughout 1943 Cunningham enhanced his reputation and gained the nickname 'Cat's Eyes'. Attributed by the press to eating carrots which, it was said, gave him great night vision, the reality was that it was good cover for the secret radar systems being developed and carried by aircraft such as the RAF night fighters.

Cunningham's next visit to Hatfield was in 1944 when he was Group Captain in charge of night operations. Having evaluated the Vampire night fighter Cunningham was amazed by the potential of the jet engine and made up his mind to join de Havilland again permanently after the war.

He duly rejoined in December 1945 again working for Geoffrey Jr. However when Geoffrey was killed in the DH108 Swallow in 1946, Cunningham became chief test pilot and immersed himself in every aspect of the Comet's development.

It is the day of the first flight and John Cunningham finds time for a publicity shot from the Comet prototype's cockpit. (BAE SYSTEMS)

It was Cunningham who flew the Horsa glider married with the Comet nose. He trained to fly on trans-Atlantic airliners to test routes and conditions. He even tested various other airliners to find which configuration would work for the cockpit. Consequently, when the time came, it was Cunningham who first flew the Comet.

# CHAPTER 3

# Into Service

SO HERE WAS this brand-new jet airliner packed with innovative features and creating headlines round the world. But it was still a long way from being ready for service with BOAC, its maiden customer.

For the few weeks after the maiden flight Cunningham and his crew were kept busy going faster, further and higher until they reached what would become normal operating speed, range and altitude. The aircraft kept performing beautifully.

BOAC's specification was for very luxurious cabins to hold thirty-six passengers and, when you consider that the Comet was only two feet shorter than a Boeing 737, which, a few years later, could carry more than 100 passengers, there was plenty of room for all the luxuries that long-distance first-class passengers could expect.

First of all, courtesy of its jet engines the Comet provided a quiet and vibration-free journey, not something usually enjoyed by passengers using piston-engine

The Comet prototype in flight on 5 August 1949. (BAE SYSTEMS)

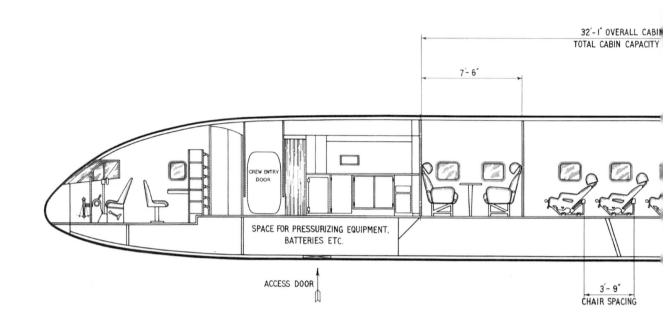

32'-1" OVERALL CABIN
TOTAL CABIN CAPACITY

7'-6"

CREW ENTRY
DOOR

SPACE FOR PRESSURIZING EQUIPMENT,
BATTERIES ETC.

ACCESS DOOR

3'-9"
CHAIR SPACING

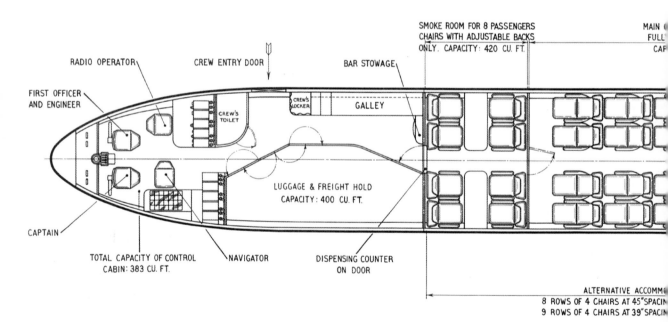

SMOKE ROOM FOR 8 PASSENGERS
CHAIRS WITH ADJUSTABLE BACKS
ONLY. CAPACITY: 420 CU. FT.

MAIN
FULL
CAP

RADIO OPERATOR

CREW ENTRY DOOR

BAR STOWAGE

FIRST OFFICER
AND ENGINEER

CREW'S
LOCKER

CREW'S
TOILET

GALLEY

LUGGAGE & FREIGHT HOLD
CAPACITY: 400 CU. FT.

CAPTAIN

TOTAL CAPACITY OF CONTROL
CABIN: 383 CU. FT.

NAVIGATOR

DISPENSING COUNTER
ON DOOR

ALTERNATIVE ACCOMM
8 ROWS OF 4 CHAIRS AT 45"SPACIN
9 ROWS OF 4 CHAIRS AT 39"SPACIN

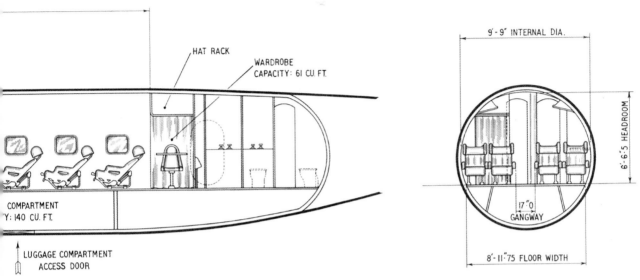

HAT RACK

WARDROBE
CAPACITY: 61 CU. FT.

COMPARTMENT
Y: 140 CU. FT.

LUGGAGE COMPARTMENT
ACCESS DOOR

9'- 9" INTERNAL DIA.

6'- 6".5 HEADROOM

17"·0
GANGWAY

8'- 11".75 FLOOR WIDTH

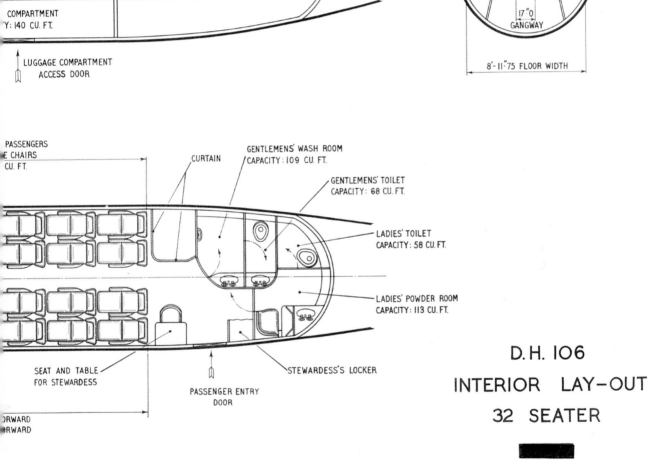

PASSENGERS
E CHAIRS
CU. FT.

CURTAIN

GENTLEMENS' WASH ROOM
CAPACITY: 109 CU. FT.

GENTLEMENS' TOILET
CAPACITY: 68 CU. FT.

LADIES' TOILET
CAPACITY: 58 CU. FT.

LADIES' POWDER ROOM
CAPACITY: 113 CU. FT.

SEAT AND TABLE
FOR STEWARDESS

PASSENGER ENTRY
DOOR

STEWARDESS'S LOCKER

ORWARD
RWARD

# D. H. 106
# INTERIOR  LAY–OUT
# 32  SEATER

aircraft. A publicity feature was made of this showing a child able to balance a pencil on end while the aircraft was in flight.

The Comet was also fast. When BOAC started jet services to South Africa in 1952 the journey time was slashed by four hours. This was achieved despite a 1,000 mile (1,609km) longer trip than the piston-engine Handley Page Hermes that was plying the route at the time, and included five stops for fresh crews or fuel.

But if the aircraft itself was packed with all the latest technology, offering smooth and fast flying, the interior revisited an earlier time of flying for an elite. BOAC went out of its way to ensure that the quality of the decor was promoted.

The Comet interior was very luxurious with the aviation journal *Flight* describing it as 'a perfect complement to the beauty of the machine'. The BOAC publicity at the time stated that 'every detail of the interior has been designed to ensure maximum comfort for the 36 passengers', and that 'the pressurised and air-conditioned cabins are fitted with super-comfortable "Slumberseats".'

A de Havilland publicity shot showing the vibration-free experience to be enjoyed by a Comet passenger. Even a house of cards stays up in a Comet! (BAE SYSTEMS)

Famous aviation journalist and photographer John Stroud recreates the famous 'pencil' shot on a flight on a Comet from London to Rome. (John Stroud Collection at AFH)

Before the arrival of the Comet, BOAC used the Handley Page Hermes on the route to South Africa, one of which is seen here on 28 December 1950. (John Stroud Collection at AFH)

The dark blue seats were set off by restful grey ceilings and walls. Available leg room on the Comet would be envied by all but current users of the best executive jets. And there was a bewildering range of men's and ladies' toilets, a 'powder room' for the ladies and a 'dressing room' for the gentlemen, coat-hanging space, a library, and, of course, a pantry for the fine food available on board.

However the Comet was not a cheap way to travel. A return trip to South Africa cost £315, a small fortune considering that a man's average salary in the UK at the time was £9 per week and a woman's was just £5. But then air travel was expensive and however costly this seemed it was no more than a standard trip via the piston-engine Hermes. Imagine if British Airways had chosen to charge the same amount for crossing the Atlantic in Concorde as in a Boeing 747!

Before BOAC could fly a single mile there was much more testing to be done. The public got its first view of the new Comet at the SBAC show at Farnborough in September 1949. Also at the show were other designs that had evolved from the Brabazon Committee's work; the Bristol Brabazon itself, the Airspeed Ambassador and the Vickers Viscount.

For the next eighteen months Comet G-ALVG undertook range and fuel consumption test flights, initially in the temperate climates of Europe but subsequently to the hot and high airports of Nairobi and Khartoum, both being

A de Havilland publicity shot of the luxurious seating to be used for dining in the Comet 1. (BAE SYSTEMS)

*Above and below:* Two mocked-up publicity shots showing the interior of the Comet 1's passenger cabin (BAE SYSTEMS)

planned stops for the Comet route to South Africa. In January 1950 the first pressurised high altitude test took place with the aircraft reaching 40,000 feet (12,192m) for the first time. The Comet also broke the London-Rome-London and London-Cairo time records.

Meanwhile the second Comet prototype, G-5-2 or G-ALZK, completed its first flight in July 1950. After initial testing it was loaned to BOAC. This meant that BOAC, pending the arrival of the first production aircraft, could begin its own testing for the thousands of elements that were required in a successful operational airline service. Based at the Operational Development Unit at Hurn airport, BOAC tested radio and navigation aids and created all the procedures for working with Air Traffic Control. Meanwhile reserve fuel requirements and emergency procedures were agreed and diversion airports that could handle the new jet were confirmed.

BOAC then began its own series of long-distance proving flights flying as far south as Entebbe in Uganda and as far east as Singapore.

Senior BOAC Captain Michael Majendie had worked alongside John Cunningham as a test pilot and was instrumental in the training of future Comet

Both Comet 1 prototypes, G-ALZK (right) and G-ALVG (left), at Hatfield in July 1950. (BAE SYSTEMS)

crews for the airline. Ground crew worked closely with de Havilland's engineers as they came to terms with the radical changes in procedures.

All through these tests the aircraft performed virtually problem-free. This was important, not only to prove to key clients such as BOAC that the aircraft would be safe and economical, but also to show doubting airlines round the world that they should be considering the jet-powered Comet for their next purchase.

In March 1952 after much rigorous testing the first production Comet 1 was delivered to BOAC. It was testament to the de Havilland team members that they had been so confident in the success of the prototype that they had pressed the button on production very early. In fact, at the time of the first flight in July 1949 there were already a number of production airframes under construction.

The new Comet was ready for the skies.

The first ever commercial jet flight was undertaken by BOAC's Comet 1 G-ALYP on 2 May 1952. The ultimate destination was Johannesburg in South Africa, with five planned stops in Rome, Beirut, Khartoum, Entebbe and Livingstone. The aircraft carried thirty-six passengers, seven crew and thirty bags of mail on a momentous 7,000-mile (11,265km) journey.

Comet 1 production aircraft G-ALYP and YR in various stages of completion at Hatfield on 1 July 1951. (BAE SYSTEMS)

BOAC crews training on the simulated cockpit in April 1952. (BAE SYSTEMS)

Comet 1 G-ALYS at London Airport on 31 January 1952. (BAE SYSTEMS)

A large contingent of de Havilland personnel, including Geoffrey de Havilland and John Cunningham, were at London Airport as 'Yoke Peter' took off at 3.12pm with Captain Majendie at the controls. He flew the legs to Rome and Beirut before handing over to Captain Marsden who took the aircraft as far as Khartoum. It would be Captain Alabaster who would take the Comet on to South Africa.

Comet 1 G-ALYS at Khartoum during 'hot and high' trials on 7 April 1952. (BAE SYSTEMS)

*Above, below and opposite top:* Three classic shots of passengers embarking on Comet 1 G-ALYP for the first scheduled commercial jet service on 2 May 1952. (BAE SYSTEMS)

Among the many well-wishers at London Airport to see the Comet off on her first commercial jet service were Sir Geoffrey de Havilland (left) and John Cunningham (second left). (BAE SYSTEMS)

Despite headwinds on the first leg to Rome, time was made up on the Beirut leg and when the Comet finally landed at Palmiefontein Airport in Johannesburg at 2.38pm GMT the following day it was two minutes early, the captain having had to kill time on the way from Livingstone. A huge crowd of close to 20,000 people packed the airport to watch this first ever scheduled commercial jet landing. A local newspaper, *The Star*, reported that cars had jammed the airport approaches as everyone wanted to see the historic event.

An AAP reporter from Australia wrote that he, along with the paying passengers, had 'relaxed luxuriously in the dove-grey and dark-blue pressurised cabin as the Comet, hurtling along at more than 230 yards (210m) a second, created an impression of motionless suspension'.

One of the passengers was a Lincolnshire man, Albert Henshaw, who had been flying since the First World War. He claimed: 'This may be as near to heaven as I'll ever get – and it's well worth it.'

Comet 1 G-ALYP after arrival at Tokyo for the first time in July 1952. (BAE SYSTEMS)

In fact there was universal acclaim for de Havilland's and BOAC's new jet airliner. Its achievements meant that there was a number of US manufacturers scratching their heads at the extent of the lead Britain now possessed in commercial jet aviation.

By June the Comet was flying to South Africa three times each week. On 11 August BOAC flew its inaugural jet service to Colombo, Ceylon. Once a week the Comet would fly via Rome, Beirut, Bahrain and Karachi, a twenty-one-hour, thirty-five-minute flight, which was a staggering eight hours shorter than the time taken by Canadair Argonauts on the same route. Before the end of 1952 Comets were flying twice-weekly to Singapore; Tokyo was added the following year.

The whole enterprise had been assisted by de Havilland's phenomenal production and testing plans for BOAC's Comets. G-ALYP had first flown in January 1951 and by January 1952 the company were six months ahead of schedule. In fact the last of the nine Comets was already in service on BOAC's South American routes by September 1952.

Surely nothing could stop the inevitable success of the Comet.

Huge crowds queued at Tokyo Haneda airport to see Comet 1 G-ALYP on 8 July 1952. (Asahi)

# CHAPTER 4

# The Comet Spreads its Wings

THE YEAR 1952 was a great one for the Comet. BOAC carried 27,700 passengers, almost exactly ten per cent of all traffic carried by the airline, with aircraft an average of 80% full. With a break-even of just 66% it meant that the Comet services were profitable in their first year. Orders from overseas were building but de Havilland knew that its US competitors would soon be developing their own jet projects.

At the end of October Boeing finally announced its first jet airliner, the 367-80, later to become the 707. The press release reported that the prototype was already

Boeing 367-80 N70700, the prototype for the Boeing 707. (Private Collection)

being constructed at Boeing's Renton factory, near Seattle in Washington State, and was expected to fly in less than two years with production aircraft deliveries beginning in 1956.

The newspapers described it as Boeing's 'Comet killer' but for Boeing it was a massive gamble. For a company that was used to virtually everything they produced being financed by the US military, 'going it alone' on a major new project with no guaranteed buyers was a huge decision. However the US Air Force quickly came to Boeing's aid, with its first orders for the C-135 family of transports and tankers being placed in 1954. The C-135 was shorter and narrower but still based on the 367-80. Many of the 800+ built are still in service today.

While Boeing at least had experience of large jet aircraft for the military, thanks to the B-47 Stratojet and the B-52 Stratofortress, Douglas Aircraft had only built a few experimental single-seat military jets and their largest production for a jet aircraft, the A-4 Skyhawk, was still some time away. However Donald Douglas decided that the company should join their competition and proposed what would become the DC-8. Both Boeing and Douglas' developments, however, were well behind the Comet.

By this time de Havilland's order book was bulging. After BOAC's Comet 1s the plan was to build upgraded aircraft; first the Comet 1A and then the Comet 2 which was expected to gain the bulk of future orders. The 1A had seating for forty-four passengers and uprated de Havilland Ghost engines. The first customer for these Comet 1As was Canadian Pacific, which was looking to get a step up on their main Canadian rival Trans Canada Airlines. The Comet 1As were destined to fly the Honolulu to Sydney route until a further order for the Comet 2 was delivered.

An early Boeing C-135 Stratolifter operating with the Military Air Transport Service of the US Air Force in 1963. (AFH)

A model of the future Douglas jet transport, the DC-8. (Private Collection)

Comet 1A CF-CUN *Empress of Hawaii*, the first delivery to Canadian Pacific, prepares for take-off from a misty Hatfield. (BAE SYSTEMS)

Overseas National Airways was another potential customer but when they failed to confirm their order Air France took their place in the queue. However it was another French airline, Union Aeromaritime de Transport (UAT), which became the second operator of the Comet when it took delivery of three 1As and used them on routes from Paris to Dakar and Casablanca. The final customer for the Comet 1A was the Royal Canadian Air Force.

So twenty-two Comet 1 or 1A variants were either delivered or on order and plans were well ahead for the Comet 2 and, eventually, the Comet 3. It was these that excited potential US customers.

US airlines had a wide variety of home-grown airliners to choose from in the early years after the war. Military giant Boeing was still a fairly small commercial airliner manufacturer, mainly of the Stratocruiser. Lockheed was making waves and growing rapidly with the graceful Constellation, but Douglas was a huge supplier of airliners with over 1,000 of their ubiquitous DC-4 and DC-6 propliners already in service, with the DC-7 due to join them in 1953.

The US government gave their manufacturers protection by subsidising airline purchases of US airliners. This made it completely impractical for a US airline to buy anything built abroad unless there was no equivalent available in the USA. It was, therefore, the Comet that gave a British manufacturer the opportunity to put their shoe in the door of the US market for the first time.

*Below and next page, top*: A pair of promotional leaflets issued by Union Aeromaritime de Transport publicising their new Comet routes; Dakar in February 1953 and Casablanca soon after. (Private Collection)

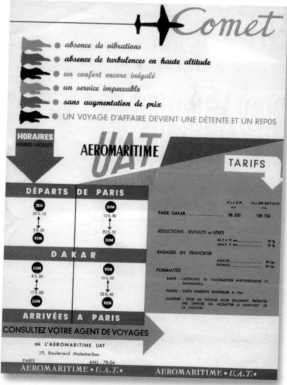

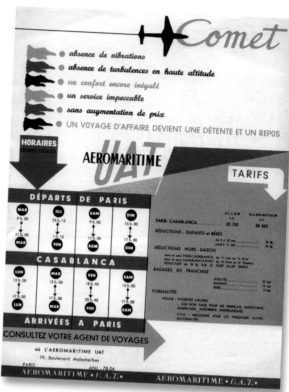

The Stratocruiser, Boeing's final piston-engine airliner. Seen here is Pan Am's N1028V *Clipper Flying Cloud* on the type's first visit to London Airport in April 1949. (John Stroud Collection at AFH)

Lockheed's graceful Constellation. This is L749A N6003C of TWA at Chicago in 1966. (AFH)

In the 1950s the skies were full of Douglas aircraft. Here is Pan Am's DC-6B N5118V at Beirut airport in 1958. (John Stroud Collection at AFH)

Cyril Lovesey, head of the Rolls-Royce design team for the Avon engine that would power all Comets from the 2 onwards. (Rolls-Royce)

This happened in October 1952 when Pan Am surprisingly made the news by announcing it had ordered three of the planned Comet 3s with an option for a further seven. The plan was to operate them on the profitable trans-Atlantic service. This order may have been simply in case Douglas or Boeing had problems with manufacturing their DC-8 and 707, but it provided a US seal of approval on the Comet project and gave hope to de Havilland that more US airlines might follow – especially when executives from TWA were seen visiting Hatfield.

There were also orders from JAL in Japan, LAV in Venezuela, British Commonwealth Pacific Airlines in Australia and, after a major charm offensive by BOAC Chairman Sir Miles Thomas and Transport Minister Alan Lennox-Boyd in 1953, Panair do Brasil ordered four. To top up the numbers BOAC ordered a further eleven Comet 2s. All in all a very healthy order book for de Havilland.

One of the key elements in the development phase was the introduction of a new engine for future Comets. The Rolls-Royce

An Avon RA9 engine about to be fitted in Comet 2X G-ALYT for testing in 1953. (BAE SYSTEMS)

Avon was an axial flow engine that had been developed by a Rolls-Royce team under Cyril Lovesey.

Lovesey had been largely responsible for the Merlin engine's development during the Second World War and had turned his attention to the Avon after the fighting ended. The Avon was too late to power the Comet 1 but was proposed for the Comets 2 and 3. Rolls-Royce began production in 1950 with the RA.3 which was used in military aircraft such as the Canberra, the early Hunters and the Supermarine Swift. The civilian RA.7 engine, which would be used by de Havilland in the Comet 2, offered more than 7,000 lbs of thrust, and there was plenty more development left for future variants.

The first Comet flight for the Avon engine took place on 16 February 1952 on the Comet 2X prototype G-ALYT, actually a Ministry of Supply Mk.1 with four Avon engines. Satisfied with its performance de Havilland put the Comet 2 into production.

The Comet 2X G-ALYT on an early test run with its Avon engines installed in June 1952. (BAE SYSTEMS)

Comet 2X G-ALYT in flight on 17 April 1952. (BAE SYSTEMS)

While the 1A had uprated Ghost engines and an increase in passenger numbers the Comet 2 took jet development a stage further. The powerful Avons were more efficient than the Ghosts, so while there was a 46% increase in thrust, the operating costs were reduced. Better fuel consumption meant that new jet routes could be opened up - including the great prize, Europe to the US. Now the aircraft was ready to fly the Atlantic.

Meanwhile the Comet 3 was announced at the SBAC Show at Farnborough in September 1952. This time it was a different aircraft altogether. The fuselage was 15ft (4.57m) longer than the Comet 2 and a more advanced Avon engine gave a massive boost to operators' potential profit. The 3 could carry fifty-six to seventy-six passengers, depending on configuration between first and economy class, and an increased fuel load meant the total weight was increased from 120,000 lbs (54,431kg) for the Comet 2 to 150,000 lbs (68,038kg) for the Comet 3.

By the end of 1953 airlines were preparing for the delivery of their Comet 2s and there were still no rivals in the air. The Comet project however was about to be dealt a hammer blow.

Comet 3 prototype G-ANLO is tilted to facilitate its roll-out from the hangar at Hatfield in May 1954. (BAE SYSTEMS)

# CHAPTER 5

# Disaster

Comet G-ALYZ on delivery day to BOAC, 30 September 1952. (BAE SYSTEMS)

IT ALL BEGAN where it would end, with an accident in Rome. The tenth and final Comet Mk.1 was G-ALYZ, which was delivered to BOAC in September 1952. Within a month, on a regular London-Johannesburg flight, it overshot the runway at Ciampino airport in Rome as Captain Foote abandoned the take-off. There were no casualties but ten per cent of the BOAC Comet fleet had been lost in one incident.

The next accident, however, ended with all on board being killed. The first of Canadian Pacific's two Comet 1As was CF-CUN, *Empress of Hawaii*, which was leaving Karachi on a leg of its delivery flight on 3 March 1953. Like G-ALYZ it failed to take-off and crashed into a dry river bed. Among the fatalities was a team of five de Havilland technicians.

These were the first ever jet airliner human losses. Canadian Pacific cancelled their order for the second Comet. In both cases the probable cause was considered to be the pilot taking off at an angle which caused a drop in speed and a stall.

EMPRESS OF HAWAII

Comet 1A CF-CUN is handed over to the Canadian Pacific crew just two days before the fatal crash in Karachi. (BAE SYSTEMS)

The wreckage of CF-CUN spread out along the dry river bed at the end of the Karachi runway on 3 March 1953. (BAE SYSTEMS)

On 2 May, exactly a year to the date since BOAC's first service, G-ALYV was destroyed in a crash on the home leg of a flight from Singapore. Leaving Calcutta en route for Delhi the aircraft took off into an unexpected thunderstorm which, according to the subsequent enquiry, caused stress on the airframe and structural failure, either because of the strong gusts of wind or a loss of control by the pilot. All forty-three on board were killed.

In June UAT's F-BGSC ran off the end of the runway at Paris, and the following month another BOAC Comet, G-ALYR, had a taxiing accident, again at Calcutta. The local papers in India reported how the aircraft's wheels had gone off the edge of the taxiway, damaging both the undercarriage and the starboard wing. Some 7,000 gallons (31,822l) of kerosene poured from a ruptured wing, filling the 'three foot deep and 70 feet long furrow through the rain-sodden ground', turning it into a pool.

Again no-one was hurt but the *Indian Express* newspaper did raise the point that there had been three Comet accidents in India in the previous few months. In all cases there seemed to be obvious explanations. Comet operators initially continued with their regular services, but the next accidents brought them all to a standstill.

The remains of one of the Ghost engines from the crash site of BOAC's G-ALYV at Calcutta 3 May 1953. (Private Collection)

It was Sunday 10 January 1954 when G-ALYP, the aircraft that had inaugurated the London-Johannesburg route, took off on Flight 781 with experienced Comet Captain Alan Gibson at the controls. Captain Albert Meagher, a hugely experienced RAF and BOAC pilot, had flown the aircraft in from Beirut that morning, handed over to Gibson and gone to his hotel. Some hours later he was called and told that the Comet had disappeared. Meagher would later be called upon as a witness for the accident investigation as he had been the last man to fly the aircraft before it crashed.

Gibson had followed normal procedures, filing regular reports about weather and position. At around 9.50am, close to 27,000 ft (8,229m) and climbing up to standard cruising altitude of 35,000 (10,668m), Gibson was in mid message to the captain of a nearby BOAC Argonaut when the transmission abruptly stopped. Witnesses reported hearing roaring and banging before flames could be seen spiralling into the sea off the coast of the Isle of Elba.

A total of twenty-nine passengers and six crew were killed on 'Yoke Peter'. Among the casualties were ten children and the famous war reporter Chester Wilmot who was returning to the UK from a broadcasting assignment in Australia.

BOAC immediately grounded all of its remaining Comets, now reduced to a fleet of seven, and co-operated with the Air Registration Board's investigation. A wide variety of causes were considered, and other Comets were examined in detail by the Royal Aircraft Establishment at Farnborough, as well as teams from BOAC and de Havilland. The prototype, which had already flown 3,000 hours more than

BOAC Comet 1 G-ALYP at London Airport on 5 September 1953. (AFH)

'Yoke Peter', was found to have some cracks but nothing that might have caused a crash. The investigators considered fatigue in the wing, and all along were the possibilities of engine failure, control issues and weather. But at this point there was no wreckage to examine for clues.

Less than six weeks after the accident, Lord Brabazon, by then chairman of the ARB, agreed with Sir Miles Thomas that everything feasible had been done. He wrote: 'Although no definite reason for the accident has been established, modifications are being embodied to cover every possibility that imagination has suggested as a likely cause for the disaster. When these modifications are completed and have been satisfactorily flight tested, the Board sees no reason why passenger services should not be resumed.'

BOAC started flying its Comets again on 23 March but just two weeks later it happened again – and in the same general area as before. G-ALYY, 'Yoke Yoke', had completed all her modifications and had been chartered by South African Airways. She landed at Rome on 7 April and was due to take-off for Cairo again later that day. However a fault in one of the fuel gauges, along with the delay caused by a replacement part being flown out from the UK, meant that the flight to Cairo did not take-off until twenty-five hours later. It was 6.32pm on 8 April when Flight 201 finally took off.

Climbing through cloud required several position checks. These done, at 7.05pm Cairo received a message giving an ETA. Nothing more was heard.

At around 7.07pm 'Yoke Yoke' crashed into the Mediterranean Sea off the island of Stromboli killing fourteen passengers and the seven crew from SAA headed by Captain William Mostert.

Transport Minister Alan Lennox-Boyd, so instrumental in spreading the word about the Comet around the world, now withdrew the certificate of airworthiness for all Comets. The whole fleet was grounded indefinitely.

Half of the Comet 1 production was now unavailable as four had been destroyed in accidents and a fifth, YT, had been modified to carry Avon engines. Remaining Comets scattered around the world were carefully returned to the UK and airframes already in the country were made available for the investigations of both crashes.

Now both investigations ran simultaneously. 'Yoke Yoke' had crashed in an area where the depth of the sea was close to 500 fathoms (3,000 ft / 914m) and nothing was recoverable apart from what already floated on the surface. However, 'Yoke Peter' crashed in an area where the depth was between 70 and 100 fathoms (420 to 600 ft), and by the end of January specially equipped ships were in the area and recovering wreckage.

By the end of August they had brought up about 70% of the crashed aircraft, enough to bring back to Farnborough and start the painstaking process of piecing together the remains and finding the reason for the crash. Meanwhile the investigation team had been busy.

BOAC Comet 1 G-ALYY at London Airport on 30 September 1953. The loss of this aircraft finally grounded the Comet fleet. (AFH)

HMS *Wrangler* was one of the first ships to arrive on station to collect wreckage from the crash site of G-ALYP. (Private Collection)

As there were such similarities between the two crashes one of the first lines of enquiry was the possibility of explosive decompression of the cabin. Even before the wreckage had arrived, and to aid with the research, G-ALYU was fitted into a water tank at Farnborough and pressure tested continuously. After the equivalent of 3,060 flights, 1,230 actual and 1,830 under these simulated conditions, the cabin failed. The aircraft was repaired and the tests continued until it happened again.

The fuselage of Comet G-ALYU being transported through the streets of Farnborough on 7 May 1954. (BAE SYSTEMS)

*Above and left*: Two images of G-ALYU being fitted into the water tank installed for testing at Farnborough. (Private Collections)

ORIGIN OF FAILURE

G-ALYU failed in the water tank and showed the source of the metal fatigue that had caused the crashes of YP and YY. (Private Collection)

As they progressed the source of the failure became clear. As the official report stated: 'Examination of the failure provided evidence of fatigue at the point where the crack would be most likely to start, namely near the edge of the skin at the corner of the window.' From this point the investigation focused on this probable cause alone.

To back up its findings the Royal Aircraft Establishment at Farnborough had received a piece of wreckage, recovered by an Italian fishing boat, that had been identified as cabin skin containing two windows in which lay the aerials. Through detailed examination it was established that it was there that the first fracture of the cabin structure of 'Yoke Peter' had occurred.

While the investigations were ongoing the cancelled Canadian Pacific Comet 1A was registered as G-ANAV and made its first flight on 23 June 1954. It was immediately sent to Farnborough and became the flying element of the investigation. Strain gauges were attached to test the Comet and the flights were undertaken by a very experienced team lead by RAE test pilot and future Black Arrows leader, Roger Topp.

FORWARD

PORT ◄──► STARBOARD

Above and below: Two pictures showing the wreckage of G-ALYP that had been brought to Farnborough in 1954. (Private Collections)

G-ALYP

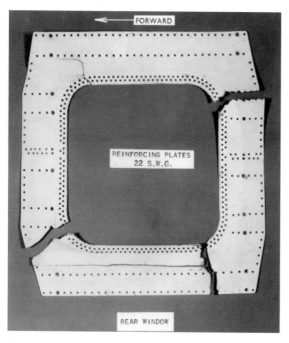

The rear ADF window on G-ALYP at which the metal fatigue caused catastrophic failure. (Private Collection)

The Court of Inquiry sat during October and November 1954. The evidence discovered during the remarkable investigation, along with testimony given by sixty-eight witnesses, left the court in no doubt. The Comet disasters had been caused by metal fatigue that had created catastrophic explosive decompression of the passenger cabin. 'Yoke Peter' had broken into a number of pieces. Death had been instantaneous for the passengers and crew as they were thrown violently around the cabin or completely clear of the aircraft at close to 30,000 ft (9,144m).

While some criticism over stress loading tests were aimed at de Havilland, no blame was attributed to anyone or any organisation. If there was any winner in this sad catalogue of events it was the process of air accident investigation. The ground-breaking report from the investigators, an exhaustive and detailed piece of work, provided the basis of how future investigations should be conducted.

What no one could answer at this point was what would happen to the whole Comet jet airliner project?

Originally registered as CF-CUM, the first Comet 1A was cancelled by Canadian Pacific and re-registered to BOAC, but then leased to South African Airways. It then became one of the Farnborough test aircraft. (AFH)

# CHAPTER 6　Comet Reborn

THROUGHOUT 1954 A regular question in aviation circles was 'Do you think the Comet will ever fly again?' De Havilland certainly believed so, as did BOAC, whose staff had been inspired by their first jet airliner and were ready for the journey to continue. There was a point when someone in government suggested that as the Comet 3 and 4 were such different aircraft the name should be changed, but the notion was rejected and the name remained.

De Havilland had announced the Comet 3 at the SBAC show at Farnborough in September 1952. It was a different aircraft from that which had gone before. It was designed for a different role with its more powerful Avon engines providing 10,000 lbs of thrust each, a fuselage that was 15 ft (4.57m) longer which meant more room for passengers and greater range with a 20% increase in fuel load.

This was the aircraft that would fly the Atlantic and had originally attracted Pan Am's order. But all orders for the Comet 3 had been cancelled after the crashes.

Unfortunately, the Comet 3 prototype, G-ANLO, was built during the crash investigations. It was too late to make some major structural changes, but it was fitted with oval windows rather than the original square ones and the engine exhausts were canted away from the fuselage allowing the hot exhausts to dissipate into the air rather than blow down the side of the fuselage. It was an improvement but it did leave one issue. The lack of structural changes meant that the aircraft could only be half pressurised so the crew had to be on oxygen for large parts of any test flight which made it uncomfortable.

De Havilland began testing on 19 July 1954. Again the first flight was under the control of John Cunningham with his long-term co-pilot Peter Bugge who had known Cunningham since they flew together in 85 Squadron during the war.

The Comet 3 was vital to the whole programme for two major reasons. Firstly because of its similarity it was able to complete much of the testing required to shorten the development process for the Comet 4. Secondly it was the only civil aircraft with the Comet name in the sky for a while and kept it in front of a world that could easily have been expected to try to forget. This was used as a way of rehabilitating and promoting the brand to a possible future audience. To this end, and to show the airliner in operation, G-ANLO undertook a massive round-the-world tour in December 1955.

One of de Havilland's biggest issues was what to do with all those Comet 2 airframes that had been built. Initially sixteen of them were modified to incorporate thicker skins and, of course, the square windows were replaced with oval ones. Thirteen that had constituted most of the BOAC order were diverted for use by the RAF at a time when they were also re-equipping with new piston-engine transports.

*Right and below.* Two photographs of the only Comet 3, G-ANLO, on the day of her first flight on 19 July 1954. The flight crew are photographed before take-off (top) and the clean lines of the Comet 3 in flight. (BAE SYSTEMS)

One of the RAF's Comet C2s in the final stages of production at Broughton in May 1957. (BAE SYSTEMS)

This immediately meant that the RAF was operating the largest fleet of jet transports anywhere in the world (see Chapter 8). One further benefit of the RAF's Comet 2s was the data provided by crews when they were debriefed by de Havilland or Rolls-Royce engineers after every flight. It all went towards the information required to complete the Comet 4 testing.

Two of the aircraft, G-AMXD and XK, were designated as Comet 2Es and modified to carry Rolls-Royce Avon 524s. With 10,500lbs of thrust this was the engine that would later be incorporated into the Comet 4 and 4B.

These two aircraft, XK now owned by BOAC while XD remained with the Ministry of Supply, were used for all the hard labour required over the next few years. They were used for engine development and testing, ensuring they would operate effectively for up to 3,500 hours. They assisted with route proving and navigation exercises in the years leading to the introduction of the Comet 4 and new crews honed their skills as they passed out from courses with de Havilland or Rolls-Royce.

Comet 2E G-AMXK being fitted with a new automatic landing system for testing in October 1962. (Smiths Group Plc)

Comet 2E G-AMXD at Beirut airport in 1957. Owned by the Ministry of Supply, but operated by BOAC, it flew daily to the Lebanon during engine trials. (John Stroud Collection at AFH)

The original first production Mk.2, G-AMXA, was used for tropical trials. In January 1954, while en route for South Africa, XA set a new record for flight time to Khartoum of just over six hours twenty-two minutes; 3,064 miles (4,931km) at an average speed of 481mph (774kph). This flight, along with others, proved that the new Comet would be ready for those trans-Atlantic crossings.

In March 1955 de Havilland announced the introduction of the Comet 4. This was followed soon after by an order for nineteen from the Comet's biggest supporter, BOAC. These aircraft would be bigger, faster, more powerful, carry a lot more passengers, and have a substantially greater range than the Comet 1. The design carried all the modifications and recommendations put forward by the Court of Inquiry.

The Comet 4 would be manufactured in two further variants. The 4B was built for BEA and was designed with a longer fuselage to carry more passengers. The final variant was the 4C, which combined the longer 4B fuselage with the wings and larger fuel tanks of the 4. This flew for the first time in October 1959 and became a favourite in the export market, tempting smaller airlines mainly in the Middle East and Central America.

Comet 2 G-AMXA during its first flight on 27 August 1953. This aircraft would become a true workhorse flying with both Nos. 51 and 216 squadrons, before undertaking trials work for Smiths Instruments. (BAE SYSTEMS)

The first production
Comet 4, G-APDA, under
final construction in
February 1958. (BAE
SYSTEMS)

Comet 4B G-APMA
undergoing trials in June
1959. This was the first
production 4B, but the
third to be delivered to
BEA. (BAE SYSTEMS)

Comet 4C G-AROV in MEA colours but never delivered. It was sold instead to Aerolineas Argentinas. (BAE SYSTEMS)

By the time the first production Comet 4 flew on 27 April 1958 more than 50,000 hours of testing, evaluating, route proving and training had been completed, substantially more than for any other aircraft before. Altogether it was estimated that the combined work done by the various Comet 2s and the Comet 3, combined with data from the RAF Comets, reduced de Havilland's and BOAC's testing time on the Comet 4 by almost two years. But there was still some work to do for BOAC's first Comet 4, G-APDA.

In the final weeks of de Havilland's testing before handing the aircraft to BOAC 'DA' flew all over the world, starting with tropical trials that took the aircraft round Africa from Khartoum and Wadi Haifa to Nairobi and Entebbe. At the end of the month it flew the Atlantic for the first time with John Cunningham inevitably at the controls. On the return leg from New York to Hatfield the crew set a new record by knocking one hour and seventeen minutes off the previous time. The flight took six hours and twenty-seven minutes.

In September, after a fleeting visit to show the Comet 4 to the public at the SBAC Show at Farnborough, more records were set while returning from Hong Kong where it helped celebrate the opening of Kai Tak airport's new

The first production Comet 4, G-APDA, takes-off for its first flight, with John Cunningham at the controls, on 27 April 1958. (BAE SYSTEMS)

John Cunningham at the controls of G-APDA ready for another test flight on 6 June 1958. (BAE SYSTEMS)

A beautiful colour shot of
G-APDA in August 1958,
just one month before
the final Certificate
of Airworthiness
was issued at the
end of September.
(BAE SYSTEMS)

G-APDA getting plenty
of interest at Khartoum
during extensive tropical
flight trials in July 1958.
(BAE SYSTEMS)

John Cunningham puts G-APDA through its paces at Farnborough during the SBAC Show in September 1958. (Private Collection)

John Cunningham being photographed by the press on 14 September 1958. (BAE SYSTEMS)

*Above and left*: Two shots of G-APDA at Kai Tak airport in Hong Kong. A visit during trials in September 1958 (top) and a commercial flight early in 1959 (bottom). (Both BAE SYSTEMS)

runway. That was 7,925 miles (12,754km) in just eighteen hours and twenty-two minutes – including two refuelling stops.

Finally Cunningham took the aircraft on a vast 'Round America' trip, north, south and central, visiting Ottawa, Gander, Toronto, the de Havilland Canada factory at Downsview, Vancouver, Mexico City, Lima, Buenos Aires, Rio de Janeiro, Caracas and New York. That trip was 23,000 miles (37,014km) in ten days.

BOAC now started the drive to bring passengers back for their new Comet. 'Flying in the Comet is like flying in a new dimension' the promotional material

John Cunningham steps from G-APDA after a flight to the de Havilland Canada factory at Downsview in Toronto on 17 September 1958. (BAE SYSTEMS)

read. It described cruising along 'steady as a rock, through dazzling sun rays or the dome of an incredibly starlit sky'. The new BOAC Sleeper-seat, 'the most sumptuous aircraft chair ever made', offered 'the most restful experience in the world' in an aircraft where 'the streamlined grace of the Comet is matched by an interior designed by one of London's leading experts' which 'creates an atmosphere at once gay and restful which will delight you'.

For the first time BOAC also offered reassurance to the passengers by describing the Comet 4 as 'the world's most tested Jetliner', the design having 'been subjected to a more intensive series of tests than any other jetliner, involving every single component of the aircraft'. The publicity also boasted that there were 'six million hours of service behind the Comet's power unit, the Rolls-Royce Avon'.

*Right*: G-APDA at Idlewild in New York on 26 September 1958. (ANP)

*Below*: Another BOAC publicity shot showing the lack of vibration in the passenger cabin, this time on the Comet 4. (Private Collection)

A gorgeous colour shot of G-APDA in flight on 1 September 1958. (BAE SYSTEMS)

The new BOAC Comet 4 was not yet ready for the world of the package holiday; that was still to come. The Comet 4 was still a first class, de-luxe, long-haul airliner designed to attract seasoned business travellers and the rich and famous.

Finally came the day they had all waited for. On 4 October 1958 BOAC's G-APDA inaugurated the London-New York Comet service flying via Gander in Newfoundland. Soon they were offering the route every day.

By 1960 all of BOAC's proposed routes for the Comet 4 were in service. Regular flights now serviced Australia, the Far East, including Hong Kong, Singapore and Tokyo, Canada and South America. In total they flew to forty-six destinations in thirty-six countries.

BOAC had beaten Pan-Am to the first trans-Atlantic regular service by just three weeks – but it did not solve their long-term problems. While BOAC's service was mainly trouble-free it was hard to compete with the Boeing 707. The Comet's six-year advantage over Boeing's new airliner had disappeared in a flurry of crashes, investigation and new development.

When the 707 entered service it brought a bigger aircraft with more powerful engines and a greater sweep to the wings which allowed faster travel over longer distances. And, although the Comet could land on shorter runways, this soon lost its relevance as airports all over the world geared up for bigger and bigger jets.

The shining nose of a brand-new aircraft, G-APDA, at London Airport in 1959. (AFH)

*Above*: John Cunningham, with Comet 4 G-APDA, surrounded by officials at Idlewild, New York, just days before the inaugural service began. (BAE SYSTEMS)

*Below left*: BOAC Comet 4 G-APDC inaugurates the first trans-Atlantic jet service on 4 October 1958. (BAE SYSTEMS)

*Below right*: As the clouds swirl in over Lion Rock, Comet 4 G-APDE arrives at Kai Tak airport in Hong Kong late in 1958. (AFH)

Comet 4 G-APDP at Singapore. (BAE SYSTEMS)

Passengers embarking on their Comet 4 as BOAC resumed services to South America in January 1960. (Private Collection)

*Above and below*: Two pictures taken at London Airport on 8 September 1958. Pan Am's Boeing 707 N709PA arrives for the type's first visit to Britain as officials are shown around Comet 4 G-APDE. (John Stroud Collection at AFH)

The Comet's resurgence at BOAC lasted barely six years. In the early 1960s the company began to sell off their aircraft. BOAC's last ever Comet service arrived back from New Zealand at Heathrow airport on 24 November 1965. By this time, BOAC was offering a full jet service via their growing fleet of Boeing 707s!

The Comet, though, was far from finished. It was about to begin its final, and perhaps most successful, role.

BOAC finally succumbed to commercial pressure and purchased Boeing 707s. G-ARWE was part of the fleet, but suffered a catastrophic fire on take-off from Heathrow in 1968. (AFH)

## G-ANLO WORLD TOUR

The plan was to take the single Comet 3 on a world tour to study its operational performance using familiar techniques on tried and tested airline routes in a wide range of climatic conditions. The aim was to prove the performance statistics for the forthcoming Comet 4. That was somewhat strange as, with typical de Havilland confidence, the statistics had already been published in a brochure distributed to all potential customers at the SBAC show at Farnborough the previous September.

Accompanying John Cunningham and co-pilot Peter Bugge on G-ANLO's round-the-world tour was a range of de Havilland executives and technicians, together with some interested observers including senior pilots from potential customer airlines.

G-ANLO at Hatfield
on 2 December 1955,
waiting for the fog to lift.
(BAE SYSTEMS)

Initially delayed by fog G-ANLO left de Havilland's Hatfield airfield on 2 December 1955. During the following twenty-six days it landed at sixteen airports in eight countries and covered a total of 27,991 miles (45,047km) in fifty-six hours and seventeen minutes' flying time.

The first stop was Cairo, followed by Bombay, Singapore and Darwin, before reaching the first major destination, Kingsford-Smith airport at Sydney. There G-ANLO was met by a crowd of more than 20,000 people awaiting their first glimpse of the new jet airliner. John Cunningham flew a number of demonstration flights to other major Australian cities before departing for New Zealand, Fiji and Honolulu.

Two days later G-ANLO left for Vancouver. It then crossed Canada, stopping at Toronto and Montreal before returning to the UK, landing at Heathrow on 28 December. Thanks to this tour G-ANLO was the first jet airliner to ever fly round the world.

The Comet 3 had made a hugely important contribution and continued to do so for the next ten years. It was modified by de Havilland and fitted with the wings destined for the Comet 4B being planned for BEA. It was then re-registered as XP915 and used by the Ministry of Supply at RAE Bedford on the Blind Landing Experimental Unit. One of its final roles was in evaluating the potential of the Comet as a maritime patroller for RAF Coastal Command. From this came the Hawker Siddeley Nimrod, the aircraft that continued the Comet concept into the 21st Century.

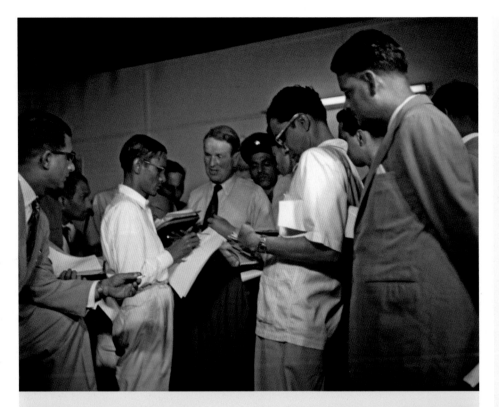

John Cunningham being questioned by the press during a refuelling stop at Bombay. (BAE SYSTEMS)

G-ANLO circling the majestic Sydney Harbour Bridge before landing on 4 December. (BAE SYSTEMS)

A slightly uncomfortable John Cunningham is welcomed to Hawaii on 13 December. (BAE SYSTEMS)

G-ANLO, in its later incarnation as XP915, attached to the RAF's Blind Landing Experimental Unit in September 1964. (AFH)

John Cunningham and co-pilot Peter Bugge being interviewed by CKWX Radio in Vancouver.
(BAE SYSTEMS)

# CHAPTER 7

# The International Comets

Comet 4 LV-PLM was the first to be delivered to Aerolineas Argentinas in 1959. (BAE SYSTEMS)

ON 22 SEPTEMBER 1958, while on its 23,000 mile (37,014km) flight round the American continents, the first Comet 4, G-APDA, landed at Buenos Aires in Argentina. While this was the first glimpse of a civil jet in that country, it was not the first opportunity Argentina's aviation experts had to evaluate the aircraft. Six months earlier a team from the Argentine Aviation Ministry and the national carrier, Aerolineas Argentinas, had arrived in the UK to consider the aircraft as the airline's first jet airliner.

The outcome of the negotiations was an order for seven aircraft, six Comet 4s and a single 4C, the final Comet variant. Initially sixteen Aerolineas crew members were trained at Hatfield and it was two of these pilots, Captains Aguirre and Llense, who flew the first aircraft back to Argentina. LV-PLM arrived at Ezeiza Airport in Buenos Aires in March 1959; all the other 4s by July 1960. At a stroke Aerolineas had become the first airline in South America to operate jet airliners – and it was the first time they had ever bought anything other than US-built aircraft.

These Comet 4s gave the company a monopoly over the South Atlantic route for two years carrying passengers to Lisbon, Rome, Frankfurt, Madrid, Paris and London. In May 1959 Aerolineas inaugurated the first weekly service to New York while also flying to destinations around South America.

This injection of power saw Aerolineas' revenues soar and the previously loss-making airline become profitable. However the airline had its fair share of problems. During the few years the Comets were in service three aircraft were lost in crashes.

Within a few weeks of services starting, on 27 August 1959 LV-AHP clipped the top of a mountain a few miles from Buenos Aires and crash-landed short of the runway. There were two fatalities; the aircraft was damaged beyond repair.

Then in February 1960 Aerolineas lost a second aircraft, LV-AHO, in a heavy landing after a training flight. With the main undercarriage legs forced up through the wings, a fire erupted which destroyed the aircraft. No-one was killed but another Comet had gone.

In November 1961 LV-AHR crashed soon after take-off from Sao Paolo airport in Brazil on a routine flight to New York. Forty passengers and twelve crew were

A publicity shot used to promote the Aerolineas Argentinas Comet services. (BAE SYSTEMS)

*Above and below.* Two shots of Aerolineas Argentinas' Comet 4 LV-AHP. In service at Dakar and after crashing at Buenos Aires on 27 August 1959. (AFH, above, and BAE SYSTEMS)

The remains of LV-AHO on 27 February 1960. (BAE SYSTEMS)

The wreckage of LV-AHR after the fatal crash near Sao Paolo in November 1961. (BAE SYSTEMS)

A further view of the wreckage of LV-AHR after its crash in November 1961. (BAE SYSTEMS)

killed. The subsequent accident investigation assumed that it was pilot error as the co-pilot was being instructed at the time.

Aside from these tragic crashes the Aerolineas Comets led a colourful life, with one being held for an unpaid debt in Paris in 1960. A second, LV-AHS, made the first round the world flight with the Argentinian president on board in 1961 while a third was hijacked to Cuba in 1970.

In 1960 East African Airways took delivery of two Comet 4s enabling it to compete with BOAC on the route from London to Nairobi. While venerable Douglas DC-3s were still plying all the internal routes their new gleaming jets were promoting the face of EAA on their long-haul routes. Two years later they received one 4C, one of the final Comets to be manufactured.

The 4C became one of the most successful Comet variants and was the aircraft that really gave the name an international feel. Mexicana was one of the oldest airlines in the world having been formed as Mexico's national carrier in 1921. It was affiliated to Pan Am in the USA – the latter owned 40% of the shares – and, although Pan Am had to select the Boeing 707 for their first jet order they funded the purchase of the Mexicana Comets in case there was an issue. This never

Comet 4C LV-AHS, of Aerolineas Argentinas, at Rome on 10 April 1964. (AFH)

Comet 4C VP-KPJ of East African Airways in flight. (BAE SYSTEMS)

A Mexicana Comet 4C, G-ARBB, seen in the hangar before re-registration as XA-NAT. (BAE SYSTEMS)

A Mexicana Comet 4C in one of the airline's promotional shots for their Golden Aztec service to various US cities. (BAE SYSTEMS)

happened, but the Comets operated successfully for almost ten years, the 'Golden Aztec' service flying to Los Angeles, Chicago and Miami regularly.

In the Middle East the largest Comet operator was Misrair, the national carrier for Egypt which was renamed United Arab Airlines (UAA) in 1960 when it undertook its short-lived merger with Syrian Airlines. The airline had a long history with de Havilland right from its early days when their first ever aircraft was a DH60 Gipsy Moth. Now their new Comets began five weekly services between Cairo and London via Rome with various stops at Geneva, Zurich or Frankfurt.

The Comets were the airline's first jets and also the first jet airliners to be operated in the Middle East. Once again the airline did not have an unbroken run of success with the type. By 1964 nine Comet 4Cs had been delivered, but President Nasser's attempts to stamp his own brand of socialism on Egypt upset the West and tourism collapsed. UAA was left with little money to maintain the aircraft and five were lost in accidents arouond the world. The Six-Day War in 1967, and the subsequent discrediting of Nasser's socialist plans, meant that business revived though the Comets were retired in 1971.

Middle East Airlines (MEA) ordered an initial four Comet 4Cs which were delivered in 1960 and 1961, being based out of Beirut in the Lebanon. Comet services were heavily curtailed when three were destroyed on the ground in Beirut. On 26 December 1968 terrorists from the Lebanese-based Popular Front for the Liberation of Palestine attacked an El Al Boeing 707 at Athens airport. Just two days later, in retaliation for the attack, Israeli commandos, arriving in eight Super Frelon helicopters, set fire to and destroyed fourteen Lebanese aircraft on the tarmac at Beirut. Among them were the three MEA Comets. MEA attempted to use leased Kuwait Comets to resume operations but by 1971 they had all been retired.

Mexicana Comet 4C XA-NAR preparing for take-off at Los Angeles in September 1964. (AFH)

President Nasser launches the new Comet service for United Arab Airlines in September 1960. (BAE SYSTEMS)

Promoting the new Comet service from the United Arab Airlines trade stand. (Private Collection)

United Arab Airlines' Comet 4C SU-ALE after crashing on snowy ground at Munich on 9 February 1970. (AFH)

Misrair Comet 4C SU-ALC rebranded after the end of the short lived United Arab Airlines merger with Syrian Airlines. (BAE SYSTEMS)

MEA Comet 4C OD-ADR under construction on 28 July 1960. (BAE SYSTEMS)

Comet 4C OD-ADQ seen on 17 April 1963. (BAE SYSTEMS)

Two other airlines to operate the Comet 4C were Sudan Airways, which received two towards the end of 1962, and Kuwait Airways, which used its two new Comets for familiarisation on jets before Tridents were delivered in 1966. The Comets had already been withdrawn from service when MEA leased them at the end of 1968. Kuwait was de Havilland's final Comet customer.

Comet 4C OD-ADT at MEA's hub, Beirut, in May 1961. (AFH)

Kuwait Airways' advertisement hoarding for their Comet service in 1963. (BAE SYSTEMS)

Kuwait Airways Comet
4 G-APDS at London
Airport in 1963. (AFH)

Sudan Airways Comet
4C ST-AAW in November
1962. (BAE SYSTEMS)

In November 1965 BOAC ceased operations using its Comet 4s but there was plenty of life left in the aircraft. During the 1950s many affiliated airlines had been set up in former British Empire countries with the local government and BOAC each owning shares. These countries, which included Ceylon, Nigeria and Ghana, took ex-BOAC Comet 4s on lease, a situation that would be repeated some years later with the VC10. Five aircraft went to Malaysian Airways, later to become Malaysia-Singapore Airlines, which took on two more. Existing operators Mexicana, MEA and East African had some of the aircraft, while two ended up in Ecuador with Aerovias Ecuadorianas.

That left a further seven to be disposed of. They all went to the single largest operator of Comets for the rest of their working lives.

Sudan Airways ST-AAX at London Airport on 1 March 1963. (AFH)

BOAC Comet 4 G-APDM at London Airport on 4 June 1959. (AFH)

At a similar location, but five years later, is ex-BOAC Comet 4 G-APDN under license to Air Ceylon. (AFH)

Ex-BOAC Comet 4 G-APDA operated by Ghana Airways in April 1961. (AFH)

Malaysian Airways' Comet 4 9M-AOE at Singapore in December 1965. (AFH)

# THE SHORT LIFE OF SA-R-7

In August 1962 a Comet 4C, registered as SA-R-7, was delivered to the Saudi Royal family to become the personal jet of King Saud bin Abdul Aziz.

The aircraft was very specially designed, as befitted a king, and featured an entire VIP cabin with luxurious seating that turned into a double bed, as well as wardrobes, a dressing room and even a special position for the private secretary.

The aircraft was based for most of the first few months in London while crew training took place, before relocating to Geneva. On 20 March 1963 the aircraft left Geneva en

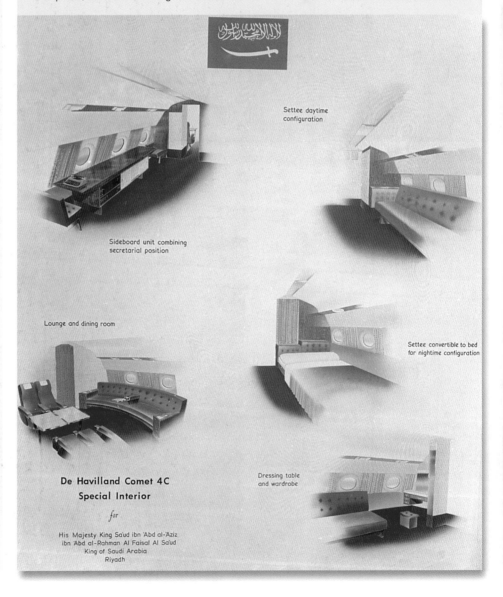

Settee daytime configuration

Sideboard unit combining secretarial position

Lounge and dining room

Settee convertible to bed for nighttime configuration

Dressing table and wardrobe

**De Havilland Comet 4C
Special Interior**

*for*

His Majesty King Sa'ud ibn 'Abd al-'Aziz
ibn 'Abd al-Rahman Al Faisal Al Sa'ud
King of Saudi Arabia
Riyadh

Some of the interior designs used for the fitting out of SA-R-7 in 1962. (BAE SYSTEMS)

SA-R-7 at Beirut on 23
September 1962, soon
after delivery. (AFH)

A rare colour shot
of SA-R-7 taken
on 29 March 1962.
(BAE SYSTEMS)

route to Nice, a relatively straightforward thirty-minute flight. On board were eighteen crew and passengers. The crew consisted of four American Saudi Arabian Airlines personnel captained by de Havilland production test pilot John Hanslip. There were two further de Havilland employees and two cabin crew together with a number of King Saud's retinue.

The aircraft crashed into the base of the Punta Bifida, just over the Italian border south-west of Cuneo, at approximately 9,000 ft (2,700m) in the middle of the night. There were no survivors. So severe was the explosion and subsequent fire that the surrounding rocks were seared by the heat. Bad weather precluded any attempt to reach the aircraft until more than five weeks later.

To this day there has never been any proper explanation offered as to why the aircraft crashed. There was a suggestion that it had been sabotaged, perhaps mistakenly thinking that the King or other members of the royal family were on board. Bad weather may have had a major effect but the total destruction of the aircraft and an unexplained drift in the aircraft's course have left open plenty of probable causes.

Fitting out for the Saudi Royal family was completed in June 1962. (BAE SYSTEMS)

# CHAPTER 8

# The Short-Haul Comet

A de Havilland model, built in 1956, showing what a Capital Airlines' Comet would have looked like. (BAE SYSTEMS)

ON 24 JULY 1956 it was announced that Capital Airlines in the USA had placed an order for four Comet 4s and ten 4As.

This was an important development for two reasons. First, Capital had never shown interest in the type before, so this would mean de Havilland extending its reach to a brand-new customer. Secondly, and perhaps more importantly for de Havilland's long terms plans, Capital was a domestic US operator, not competing on international and trans-Atlantic routes instead offering services on key internal routes such as Washington-Chicago and as such not needing the long-haul Comet.

Capital was already operating a substantial fleet of Vickers Viscount 700s and now their jet aircraft of choice was the proposed short-haul Comet variant, the 4A. This meant an aircraft suited to lower cruising altitudes, higher speed and more passengers. The 4A was to have a shortened wingspan of 108 feet and a stretched fuselage that allowed ninety-two passengers to be carried.

But de Havilland's search for a US customer was to continue. Capital was expanding too fast and could not earn enough to finance the new aircraft purchase. Further financial troubles led to a takeover by United Airlines in 1961 and the final cancellation of the Comet order.

However not everything was lost. The 4A would soon become the 4B and this new variant's major customer became British European Airways. The 4B would be the biggest Comet yet carrying up to 102 passengers. BEA ordered an initial six 4Bs and had options to take up to another eight.

The plan was for de Havilland to deliver the first 4B on 1 January 1960 but, as with all previous Comet orders, they were ahead of the game. The first, G-APMB, arrived at Stansted airport on 9 November 1959 and the first seven aircraft were all in BEA's hands by July 1960. So why seven rather than six?

BEA wanted to use Comets on roughly a quarter of all its services, approximately the same workload as for the much larger BEA Viscount fleet. This was a very heavy schedule and would fully utilise all six aircraft with no standby available. BEA had recently concluded a partnership with Olympic Airways in Greece, and Olympic had leased two Comet 4Bs from BEA, followed later by its own order for two further Comets. But to fulfill both companies' joint and individual services there was need for another aircraft in case of unserviceability.

One of Capital Airlines' large fleet of Viscount 700s. This is N7409 at Chicago in May 1961. (AFH)

*Above and below:* Two of BEA's first Comet 4Bs attracting attention from the crowds. G-APMA (top) in July 1959, and G-APMB (bottom) in September. (Both BAE SYSTEMS)

A great ground view of activity round one of BEA's Comet 4Bs. (BAE SYSTEMS)

G-AOYI, seen here at Dublin in 1968, was one of the substantial Viscount fleet operated by BEA (AFH)

A beautifully restored shot of Olympic Airways Comet 4B G-APYC in April 1960. (BAE SYSTEMS)

De Havilland and BEA worked closely together on the delivery as BEA had also ordered twenty-four DH121 Tridents, described at that point as 'second generation jets'. The original plan was for BEA to buy the Comets and operate them for four years before handing them back in return for the new Tridents. Together with another new fleet of twenty Vickers Vanguards a lot was expected from the BEA sales team in promoting the airline to fill all the available seats.

On 1 April 1960 three Comet services would start. While Moscow and Warsaw would be twice-weekly the key route would be London-Athens, via Paris or Rome, operating in tandem with Olympic Airways.

Athens would become the hub for all eastern Mediterranean destinations including Beirut, Cairo, Tel Aviv, Nicosia and Istanbul. Later in the year BEA's destination list for its Comets would include Zurich, Dusseldorf, Frankfurt, Nice, Copenhagen, Oslo and Stockholm.

It is easy to see that this was not a series of traditional holiday destinations. At this point it was too soon for BEA to develop carrying package holiday tourists so this was a short-haul European version of the service offered by BOAC.

*Above*: BEA Vickers Vanguard G-APEE seen here in Sicily in March 1961 inaugurating the first weekly London-Sicily service. (AFH)

*Below*: De Havilland Trident 1 G-ARPA seen at London Airport on 22 August 1965. (AFH)

*Right and below:* Two of BEA's Comet service destinations. G-APMB at Moscow in 1960 (top) and G-APMA at the original Athens Hellinikon airport in July 1959. (Both BAE SYSTEMS)

G-APMB at Zurich in 1960. (BAE SYSTEMS)

A BEA Comet promotional brochure shows the range of destinations all over Europe. (Private Collection)

BEA executives enjoying a BEA Comet 4B passenger cabin in November 1959. (BAE SYSTEMS)

As with the BOAC Comet 4s BEA promoted the 4B's comfort, speed and safety. Flying at a cruising speed of 530mph, and at a height of 25,000 feet, the 4B could fly London-Rome in only two hours, ten minutes; Rome-Athens was just one hour, forty-five minutes; and Moscow three hours, twenty-five minutes. The airline made them instantly recognisable with its striking new livery which included the BEA emblem on the tail and fuselage while the wings were painted almost entirely red.

Apart from the four aircraft that eventually went to Olympic Airways, BEA was the sole customer for the 4B. However by the late 1960s the aircraft was becoming less competitive, especially against the growing charter industry mainly carrying British holidaymakers to the Mediterranean resorts.

The Civil Aviation (Licensing) Act of 1960 set up the Air Transport Licensing Board to which British airlines had to apply for licenses if they wanted to operate air routes. During the 1960s more and more new companies applied for these licenses. It was the charter flights, those non-scheduled services, which grew three times faster than scheduled operations.

And so in 1969 BEA decided to set up its own charter operation. Based at London Gatwick airport rather than Heathrow, BEA Airtours started operating charter services all over Europe from March 1970. Its aircraft were nine of the ex-BEA Comet 4Bs which had been transferred from the parent company.

Not satisfied with this expansion BEA also set up a number of package tour holiday companies such as Sovereign and Enterprise. And to complete the group, BEA, along with BOAC, became instrumental in bringing overseas tourists to Britain through Windsor Tours which became one of the most successful package tour operators offering holidays in the UK.

In its first year alone BEA Airtours carried more than 650,000 passengers with Palma in Majorca as the most popular destination. However nine aircraft could not sustain this level of activity for long. More aircraft were needed – and they had to be bigger.

By 1972 BEA Airtours had acquired two of BOAC's Boeing 707s. Within two more years the entire fleet was 707s. The Comets had been passed on to what would become their final chapters in British commercial aviation.

Four Comets had very short-lived careers in Channel Airways but when it ceased operating in 1972 they were passed on to Dan-Air, which would become the operator of the single largest fleet of Comets and take the aircraft into its final retirement.

Dan-Air was created almost by accident in 1953 when a debt, owed by Meredith Air Transport to ship and aircraft broker Davies and Newman, was settled with the handing over of their aircraft and the contracts to run a single Douglas DC-3 from Southend to Tempelhof in West Berlin. From this small start Dan-Air became

A promotional shot of Comet 4B G-APMG in July 1960. (BAE SYSTEMS)

*Above and below*: Two pictures of BEA Airtours Comets. Above is Comet 4B G-ARJK at Manchester in the height of the holiday season in August 1970, while below is Comet 4C G-ARJL. (Both AFH)

*Above and below*: Into the 1970s and aircraft are changing. Above is the ex-BEA Comet 4B G-APZM, seen at Manchester wearing Channel Airways livery in 1971, while below is a BEA Airtours 707, G-APFL, at Gatwick in 1973. (AFH)

Dan-Air's original Douglas DC-3 G-AMSU seen at London Airport in 1965. (AFH)

an almost unique airline that remained profitable for thirty-seven years until its last few years of decline, eventually being sold to British Airways in 1992.

Key to Dan-Air's success was its ability to buy better value second-hand aircraft. They never felt the need to buy new and therefore expensive aircraft such as the BAC1-11 or Boeing 737 that were operated by so many other charter companies. They just waited until they became surplus to requirements elsewhere. And so when Dan-Air decided to expand into the jet market, it coincided with the slow but regular retirement of Comets from Britain's premier airlines.

Dan-Air's substantial fleet of Comets, forty-eight overall, was acquired from BOAC, BEA, Channel Airways, BEA Airtours and a number of international airlines between 1966 and 1976. Not all would be operational as a number were used for spares.

The company's first acquisitions were three ex-BOAC Comet 4s, first G-APDK and DO in 1966, with DJ added the following year. These were delivered to Dan-Air Engineering at Lasham airfield in Hampshire and converted to carry ninety-nine passengers. Though there was less space for the passenger the aircraft were generally used on shorter and much cheaper flights; Dan-Air realised passengers would settle for less if they had to pay less.

It was the end of 1968 when Dan-Air really started to build its Comet fleet. This coincided with Dan-Air retiring most of its Airspeed Ambassadors and marked the start of the company's major period of growth in aircraft, passenger numbers and routes.

With such a vast fleet the company had to make the aircraft work, so one of its plans involved setting up a second base at Tegel in West Berlin and offering the same type of service to the West German people. In March 1968 a Comet left Tegel for Malaga in southern Spain, the first of many over the next few years that would offer a mix of scheduled and charter flights.

The Comets were used on many Dan-Air routes during the late 1960s and 1970s. One Comet might be flying across the Atlantic while another flew the daily Gatwick-Newcastle service. That was the benefit of having a mix of long and short-haul Comets in the fleet. Dan-Air also set a record when it became the first airline to employ a woman as a jet captain when Yvonne Sintes became a BAC 1-11 and Comet captain in 1975.

During the 1970s Dan-Air's passenger numbers grew rapidly. From 500,000 in 1969 it flew 1,000,000 in 1971. This number kept doubling until 1978 when 4,000,000 flew with the airline. By this time the Comets had been joined by Boeing 727s and BAC 1-11s and were nearing the end of their service lives.

Dan-Air always tried to offer a more personal and friendly service, often tailoring food to particular seasons. Altogether it had a good reputation among the travelling public. Unfortunately it suffered its own share of aircraft losses, including one of their Comets. In July 1970 ex-BOAC Comet 4 G-APDN crashed into a hillside near Barcelona while on charter with Clarkson's Holidays. Commanded by Captain Alex Neal it was a regular flight from Manchester to Barcelona. All 105 passengers and seven crew were killed.

By the mid-1970s the Comet fleet was coming under the spotlight. The 1974 fuel crisis highlighted the type's lack of efficiency, especially when compared to the new arrivals such as the BAC 1-11. As fuel prices rose it became harder to justify using the Comets and, although many of them had plenty of flying hours left in them, it just became too uneconomical to use this 1950s technology.

At the end of the 1970s they began to be phased out of service. Dan-Air operated the last ever commercial Comet flight when 4C G-BDIW landed at Gatwick in November 1980.

Ex-BOAC Comet 4 G-APDK in Dan-Air livery at Gatwick in May 1967. (AFH)

While Dan-Air continued to fly Comets, they also began to bring in newer aircraft. Here is the fifteen-year-old ex-RAF Comet C4 re-registered as G-BDIX at Newcastle in 1977. (AFH)

Meanwhile, they had already taken delivery of their first Boeing 727 G-BAEF in 1972. (Private Collection)

Wreckage from Comet 4 G-APDN is strewn across the hillside south of Barcelona after the crash in July 1970. (AFH)

A classic shot of Comet 4C G-BDIX. (AFH)

Just a few weeks before its final commercial flight, Dan-Air's Comet 4C G-BDIW sits at Gatwick at the end of October 1980. (AFH)

# AIRLINE FOR SALE

Westernair was an aviation dealership based at Alberquerque in New Mexico that offered for sale everything from old DC-6s and Convair CV240s to ex-military trainers and flying boats. In 1973 Westernair acquired three ex-Mexicana Comet 4Cs and offered them for sale in a complete package under the headline of 'A Complete Jet Airline for less than $1,000,000'. The three aircraft had been re-registered in the USA with XA-NAT becoming N777WA, XA-NAR now N888WA and XA-NAS as N999WA. The package included a Redifon 4C flight simulator that would cost $1,000,000 new, a total parts inventory including six spare Rolls-Royce Avon 525s, and a whole host of ground support equipment from generators and lifting equipment to a dozen tow bars.

They wanted to sell the three aircraft together with all the kit as a complete package, but there were no takers. Eventually, two of the aircraft were sold to separate customers in the United States, with N888WA ending up at the Museum of Flight in Seattle. N999WA was eventually scrapped in the 1990s. As for N777WA it was damaged during its last flight for Mexicana and never left Mexico. It still survives to this day as an attraction at the Parque Zoologico Irapuato in Mexico.

Dick Drost owned a nudist colony in Roselawn, Indiana, and bought Comet N999WA from Westernair to ferry customers to his colony. However, the aircraft broke down at Chicago's O'Hare Airport and was eventually scrapped. (AFH)

# 1960s BRITISH AIRCRAFT INDUSTRY SHENANIGANS

The 1960s was a very confusing time to be in British civil aviation. It was rife with mergers, changing specifications and requirements, and subsequent delays, fruitless negotiations with US airlines and the disappearance of many household names.

It was a time of radical changes in the aircraft industry. Negotiations were in hand to drastically reduce the number of aircraft manufacturers in Britain and to create bigger and hopefully better and more streamlined corporations that could become world contenders.

To this end two large corporations were created. The ever-decreasing number of government aircraft contracts meant that merger or acquisition was the only answer. Even before the Second World War Hawker Siddeley had become the parent company for such great names as Hawker, Gloster and Avro. Now it added Folland, de Havilland and Blackburn.

Meanwhile the formation of the British Aircraft Corporation from the merger of Hunting, Bristol, English Electric and Vickers, meant that there were now just two major fixed wing manufacturers competing for British government contracts. Fairey merged into Westland and became one of the most important helicopter manufacturers in the world while companies such as Handley Page, which resisted attempts to force a merger, was unable to compete and eventually went into voluntary liquidation in 1970.

The British aircraft industry's biggest customer by far was the British government on behalf of the various military air services and the national civil carriers, BOAC and BEA.

An example of a great aircraft built by the newly-merged BAC – BAC and Aerospatiale's majestic supersonic Concorde. (AFH)

In return they were expected to buy British and the companies were expected to create aircraft for them meaning that on many occasions the aircraft that were delivered were so tailored to specific requirements they became virtually unsaleable to any overseas air force or airline.

Another aircraft built by the newly-merged BAC – a BAC One Eleven, G-AVML, at Farnborough in 1968. (AFH)

Originated by de Havilland as the DH125, the Hawker Siddeley HS125 became a huge success selling to companies and air forces all over the world. (BAE SYSTEMS)

BAC's potential world-leading military development, TSR2, was cancelled in April 1965. (BAE SYSTEMS)

# CHAPTER 9 Comets for the RAF

THE COMET'S FIRST military operator was the Royal Canadian Air Force which had been supplied with two Comet 1As in 1953. After the 1954 crashes the aircraft were returned to the UK for modification before rejoining the RCAF. They continued to operate successfully until they were finally phased out in 1964.

In the wake of the 1954 Comet accidents orders for the Comet 2 faded away. And when de Havilland announced the Comet 4 it seemed that the part-finished Mk.2 airframes might be scrapped, something de Havilland could ill afford.

However de Havilland's subsequent decision to finish the production of sixteen of the aircraft, incorporating most of the post-crash modifications, was the correct one. Taken on by the Ministry of Supply thirteen of them were redistributed to the RAF as T.2s or C.2s and became the world's first ever military jet transports. This began a long history of the RAF operating Comets. When the C.2s began to age five new Comet 4s, known as C.4s, were ordered and joined the RAF's fleet.

This aircraft, '5302', was a Comet 1X in service with 412(T) Squadron RCAF. It is seen here at Toronto in November 1953. (BAE SYSTEMS)

*Above and right*: Two pictures of RAF Comet C2 XK695. On display at Farnborough in September 1956 (top) and at Hatfield being modified to a Mk.2R for radio signals duties (bottom). (Both BAE SYSTEMS)

This was a completely new and unexpected initiative for RAF Transport Command. It had already planned an upgrade and was waiting for two new aircraft to arrive. The Blackburn Beverley was a very effective heavy lifter while the Bristol Britannia provided a long-range trooping service starting in 1959. But neither was jet-powered.

A line-up of RAF Comets, both T2 and C2 variants, of 216 Squadron at Lyneham. (BAE SYSTEMS)

Two squadrons operated Comets during their service life. The primary transport squadron was 216 which, based at RAF Lyneham in Wiltshire, operated Comets for twenty years. Meanwhile 192 Squadron had Comets for a year before being renumbered as 51 Squadron; it continued flying its jets in 'special duties' roles until 1974 when they were replaced by the Comet-inspired Hawker Siddeley Nimrod R1.

The first two aircraft delivered to 216 Squadron were XK670 and XK669 which were both designated as T.2s for training future Comet crews. These were followed by a further eight C.2s equipped as normal transport aircraft. In February 1962 the C.2s were augmented with five new C.4s. These offered the same advantages enjoyed by BOAC in that they could carry twice as many passengers a lot further and much faster. When the C.2s were retired from service in April 1967 the C.4s carried on until 1975.

Interestingly 216 Squadron was operated much like a commercial airline. It flew to schedules delivering troops, VIPs and supplies wherever British forces were stationed around the world. The squadron ran a tight timetable which allowed it to link all the major RAF bases round the world including Cyprus, Malta, Singapore, Hong Kong and Aden. The Comets could also be reconfigured for

RAF Comet C2 XK671 is resupplied on a regular trooping trip to the Far East in June 1957.
(BAE SYSTEMS)

VIPs are served by the crew of Comet C2 XK716 on a trip to the United States in 1959. (BAE SYSTEMS)

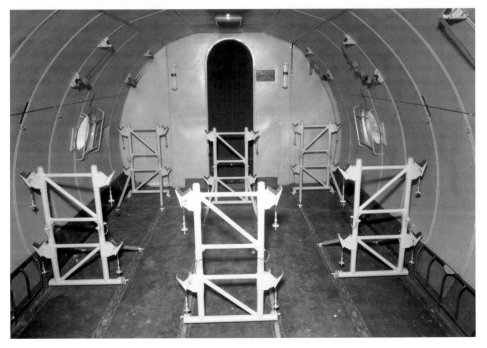

An RAF Comet C2 after conversion for carrying stretchers on a casualty evacuation operation in 1958. (BAE SYSTEMS)

An ambulance pulls up to Comet C2 XK671 to transfer casualties from the aircraft to hospital in June 1957. (BAE SYSTEMS)

casualty evacuation by the swift replacement of seats with bunks, stretchers and separate medical facilities.

The 216 Squadron ground crew were also extremely proud of their aircraft. When their Comets were sold off by the RAF to Dan-Air from 1975 the civil air and ground crews found them to be in immaculate condition despite the millions of miles flown.

Partly due to its unique position as the only jet transport squadron in the world 216 performed a myriad of tasks. A prime example of the variety of operations undertaken by the Comets was a trip to Argentina for the inauguration of the new President in February 1958.

This coincided with the time when de Havilland had just sold new Comet 4s to Aerolineas Argentinas. A C.2, XL670, was reconfigured as a VIP transport with new fittings and BOAC-style seating. The key VIP on this diplomatic mission was the Secretary of State for Air, George Ward.

It had been a tempestuous political time in Argentina after Juan Peron had been ousted in 1955, with the next three years seeing coups d'etat, arrests, demonstrations, bombing and kidnapping. The political vacuum was filled by Arturo Frondizi who had gained his position with help from Peron in exile.

Into this scenario arrived the RAF Comet together with a majestic show of force in the form of two 83 Squadron Avro Vulcans. During the visit not only

*Above and below.* Secretary of State for Air George Ward MP, on a flag-waving tour of South America in June 1960, seen at El Dorado Airport in Bogota, Colombia. His transport was Comet C2 XK697. (Private Collections)

did Her Majesty's representative attend the inauguration of the new president, but hundreds of thousands of people saw the aircraft which took part in the celebratory fly past. Journalists had the opportunity to fly in the Comet, and the Vice President of Aerolineas even took the controls for a time. Reports from the record-breaking trip showed that the Comet had enjoyed 100% serviceability and had given the people of Argentina a fine impression of Britain's aviation industry.

When the C.2s were withdrawn they had flown more than twenty-five million miles (40,233,600 km) and carried more than 380,000 passengers. The Comet C.4s proved to be no less perfect for the role as they continued with trooping commitments all over the world. When the Comets were finally retired from military service with the squadron in 1975, 216 was disbanded awaiting a radical new role.

Arturo Frondizi, the first reasonably stable President of Argentina since Juan Peron. (Private Collection)

Final planning for the next flight for Comet C2 XK698. (BAE SYSTEMS)

*Above and below*: Two great images of the new Comet C4 in RAF service. Above is XR399 in flight, with, below, XR397 at Heathrow in 1967. (BAE SYSTEMS, top, and AFH)

Less well-known were the covert operations of 51 Squadron from its bases at Wyton in Cambridgeshire and Watton in Norfolk. The aircraft operated by 51 Squadron were designated as Comet C.2R and took on the ELINT (electronic intelligence) role with the Canberra, replacing the slower piston-engine Boeing B-29 Washingtons and Avro Lincolns. This electronic intelligence role centred around the interception of signals and the monitoring of radar and missile sites. The accepted enemy was the Soviet Union so the Comets would snoop around the Baltic coast, the Barents Sea and the Black Sea, often near Soviet naval bases, and along the Soviet borders with Turkey and Germany, but rarely actually overflew enemy territory, leaving that to the USA.

It could be a dangerous job. A Lincoln had been shot down near the German border in April 1953 with the loss of the whole crew, and many ELINT flights were closely monitored by MIG fighters ensuring they never got too close to Soviet territory. Regularly the Comets would be acquired by Soviet missile batteries – but never fired on.

Cockpit layout for the Comet 2R, in this case XK655, as operated by 51 Squadron. (BAE SYSTEMS)

These aircraft were substantially refitted for their role with many aerials mounted into the skin. This meant that they could only be partially pressurised and the crew, expanded by the addition of up to ten radar specialists, would have to spend much of their flights on oxygen, wearing arctic clothing and operating at 37,000 feet.

51 Squadron only operated three C.2Rs and this was cut to two when XK663 was lost in a hangar fire at RAF Watton in June 1959. The two remaining Comets continued until replaced with Nimrod R1s in 1974.

A number of other Comets were operated by the military at various times. The Ministry of Supply and the Royal Aircraft Establishment, for example, used Comets as engine test beds as well as for testing radio and communications, guidance systems and navigation equipment. One was employed to test the planned future Nimrod AEW nose.

In fact it was an RAE aircraft that made the final ever Comet flight when XS235, named *Canopus*, took off on 14 March 1997. On board was the almost eighty-year old John Cunningham, the man who had made the Comet's first flight in July 1949.

The Comet C2 fleet stayed in service with 216 until 1967 when just the C4s remained. The aircraft in this image are T2 XK670, C2 XK698, XK695, XK69 and XK715. (BAE SYSTEMS)

The Hawker Siddeley Nimrod, which was inspired by, and based on, the Comet airframe. Sadly, this example, XV230, crashed in Kandahar, Afghanistan in September 2006 with the loss of all on board. (AFH)

The Royal Aircraft Establishment's Comet 2E XN453 landing at Farnborough in July 1969. (Private Collection)

The Comet 4 AEW testbed XW626 in flight. (Private Collection)

A&AEE's Comet 4C XS235 *Canopus* was the last Comet to fly, seen here in July 1989. (BAE SYSTEMS)

A classic close-up of the nose of *Canopus* in 1980. (AFH)

# 216 SQUADRON RAF

For most of its operational life 216 Squadron has flown transport aircraft. Initially formed on Handley Page bombers during the First World War as 'A' Squadron, and then 16 Squadron RNAS, it was renumbered as 216 Squadron, part of Trenchard's Independent Force, when the RAF was formed in 1918.

After the war 216 Squadron was posted overseas and spent virtually all of the inter-war years, and the Second World War, out of the UK. Flying passengers and air mail on the Cairo to Baghdad route, the squadron operated a variety of aircraft including the HP 0/400, Vickers Vimy, DH10 Amiens, Vickers Victoria and Vickers Valentia.

During the first years of the Second World War, still operating ageing Valentias, Bristol Bombays and even Dragon Rapides, the squadron took part in casualty evacuation, transportation and even a few small bombing raids in the eastern Mediterranean before eventually receiving Dakotas in 1943. For the rest of the war it flew all over India, Burma, East Africa, the Middle East, as well as undertaking operations over Yugoslavia in support of Tito's partisans and then British forces in the Greek civil war.

The Dakotas eventually went in 1949 to be replaced by Valettas. The squadron moved back to Britain in 1955 to prepare for the arrival of the Comets. When the Comets went in 1975 the squadron was disbanded until a short and uncharacteristic reformation flying ex-Royal Navy nuclear-capable Buccaneers on maritime strike operations in 1979.

In 1984, 216 Squadron returned to more familiar flying, operating Lockheed Tristars as tankers and transports. It was heavily involved in operations in Iraq, Kosovo, Libya and Afghanistan. The squadron was disbanded again in 2014.

A Vickers Victoria used by 216 Squadron for route proving and the regular Cairo-Baghdad mail run between the wars. (John Stroud Collection at AFH)

Vickers Valettas replaced Dakotas in 216 Squadron after the war. (AFH)

A 216 Squadron
Lockheed Tristar tanker,
in this case ZD953, at
RAF Brize Norton. (AFH)

# 51 SQUADRON RAF

From its formation in 1916, 51 Squadron undertook a number of different roles ranging from home defence and night fighting to training. Disbanded in 1919 it was reformed in 1937 as a bomber squadron and by the outbreak of war in 1939 was equipped with Armstrong Whitworth Whitleys. With these 51 Squadron took part in many of the early raids of the war until taking on a temporary transfer to Coastal Command in May 1942. Back in Bomber Command, and re-equipped with the Handley Page Halifax, crews flew as part of 4 Group for the rest of the war.

In 1945, 51 Squadron was transferred to Transport Command operating Stirlings and Yorks. It took part in the Berlin Airlift before being disbanded again in 1950.

In 1958, 192 Squadron was renumbered as 51 Squadron and took on the covert ELINT role flying Comet C.2Rs and modified Canberra B.2s and subsequently B.6s.

The squadron continued its Special Duties role replacing the Comets in 1974 with the Nimrod R1 and more recently, from 2013, the Boeing RC-135 Rivet Joint. The RAF's three RC-135Ws are highly-modified KC-135R Stratotankers packed with intelligence gathering equipment, all of which gives the squadron vital strategic and tactical roles in the RAF for the foreseeable future. At the time of writing 51 Squadron is based at RAF Waddington in Lincolnshire.

Handley Page Halifax LV857 of 51 Squadron in the last months of the war. (BAE SYSTEMS)

A 51 Squadron Boeing RC-135W Rivet Joint, known in the RAF as Airseeker, at RAF Waddington in May 2014. (© Crown Copyright/ Open Government Licence v 3.0)

# CHAPTER 10

# The Comet Experience

BRIAN BURDETT JOINED the RAF at just seventeen-and-a-half in 1952. After training he was posted to a Hunter squadron at Wattisham. When that was disbanded he spent a few months on a Hastings squadron before being asked if he wanted to fly the RAF's Comet 2s. At the age of twenty-two he was posted to 216 Squadron as a co-pilot at Lyneham in Wiltshire.

In those early days of military Comets there was no RAF training school, so Brian went to de Havilland at Hatfield for four weeks in June 1957 before joining the squadron in August. He takes up the story:

*To begin with I didn't fly it very much after the course at Hatfield, and I didn't get to handle it very much as the captain did all the take-offs and landings and I was allowed to do the work in the middle.*

*The aircraft had a very cosy and cramped cockpit, but the seats were excellent, as good as any seats I ever had in the RAF, in any aircraft actually, really comfortable. Pressurisation was important because of the history and whenever a pilot left the flight deck the other pilot had to go on oxygen.*

*The aircraft was very easy to fly, it actually handled well. The instruments were all very old fashioned and standard and the layout was pretty good but like any older aircraft there were switches here and there that didn't have any logic to their actual position.*

*As you would expect the engineer's panel was well laid out, much better than the pilot's. The navigator was behind the captain and the engineer behind the co-pilot and next to the engineer were boxes and boxes of radios and equipment. Behind that sat the signaller next to the right front door.*

*When I went back to Comets in 1963 the signaller had gone and the radio equipment had become very good but using the radios was a bit hard because of NDBs (non-directional beacons). You had to dial up NDBs and get the right code coming in and in bad weather conditions NDBs preferred to search out thunderstorms rather than beacons. But the navigators were brilliant.*

*We used to do a cruise climb and all the airways were at 25,000 ft (7,620m). So, when we started, depending on temperature and everything, the aircraft would start round about 30,000 ft (9,144m) perhaps and we would fly at Mach .74 (568mph, 914kph), set the engines at 7,400 rpm and we would rely on the autopilot to maintain the speed and as the fuel slowly burnt off so you would climb. Before the end of the trip we would easily get to 35,000 or 37,000 ft (10,668m, 11,277m).*

*Sometimes you would find you levelled off a bit, so you were constantly playing with the trim. If people walked up and down in the aircraft it went out of trim, believe it or not, so you had to use the trim wheel to set it back to central. You always knew when coffee was*

Comet C2 XK671 in flight.
(BAE SYSTEMS)

coming as it would suddenly start going nose down and you knew someone was coming from the back and once they passed the centre of gravity around the wings the nose would go down a bit faster, so you were constantly trimming.

It had a few eccentricities for example, you would take-off in what they called coarse gear, in other words your elevators were very receptive to control input and as you got higher, to a specific height, you then selected fine gear. What would happen then was the elevator was reduced in its arc of use, so you couldn't over-control the aircraft. Down below at lower speeds it didn't matter if you had the elevators wobbling around quite a bit but when you were going at high speed you didn't want great lumps of elevator going into the slipstream, so obviously you just reduced its movement and that way you couldn't overstress the aircraft.

It was pretty primitive in many ways. For example, they had no way of controlling the icing that took place inside the aircraft on the inner skin. You'd climb up and cruise for a long while and then before the descent the quartermaster would come up with towels which he would put around our shoulders and our laps because, once you started descending and the air outside was getting warmer and the heater inside was working, all the ice on the inside would start dripping all over the place. How it never caused any incidents with the electrics I have no idea, but it certainly made us wet. To show you how primitive it was we had a little tube about half an inch to an inch across all around the cockpit with little holes in and all the cool or hot air came out of there and you would put your hands over it to get them warm.

It was certainly good in bad weather, in terms of turbulence, because it was pretty stable and didn't wander around as much. I know we proved that once when we lost our radar between Karachi and Ceylon. We went through an inter tropical front and so we actually entered thunderstorms which we wouldn't have dreamed of doing had the radar been working. It was pretty bloody unpleasant and yet the aircraft took it and it was structurally very sound but we got thrown around, I'll tell you, we were never upside down but we had lots of bank on at times, just nothing we could control.

Brian retains many vivid memories of his time on the Comet 2s:

In Ceylon, Colombo, or Katunayake as it was, the runway wasn't long enough for us so they put down PSP, you know the perforated steel planking, two or three feet wide which interlocks, and what we used to do was actually land so that eventually we would go onto it at a slow speed. We liked to start our take-off from it so we could accelerate at a decently

An RAF Comet C2 takes off from one of the many hot and dry airfields along their regular routes to the Far East. (BAE SYSTEMS)

slow speed before we hit the runway concrete. If we took off towards the sea it was no big deal at all, but if we took off inland there was a big slope in front of you on that runway and there still is but now it doesn't matter because they've now cut all the trees down but when we used to take-off all we used to take-off towards was forest and we'd get airborne and we'd skin these trees.

We did a lot of flights to Woomera, a rocket range north of Adelaide where a lot of the early rockets for aircraft and for ground-to-air were developed. We used to take a lot of spares and scientists. Because there weren't enough aircraft we didn't have slip crews in those days, so we would stay with the passengers in a hotel or in the RAF base. In Karachi we were in the BOAC hotel on the airfield. In Nicosia we stayed in the mess. We didn't stay in Katunayake, we just went Karachi, Katunayake, Changi, stayed at Changi on the RAF base, then we went to Darwin, didn't stay there, and on to Adelaide where we stayed with the RAAF.

On the way back to Singapore we would have an extra day off and then we would come back via Colombo, no night stop, and then to Khormaksar which was awful. It was the most awful climate, it was so hot and sticky. Then we would go Khormaksar to El Adem, sometimes we would stop at El Adem which was near Tobruk and sometimes we would carry on up to home. But we always stayed with the passengers and when we went across the States we did the same.

The air force was pretty proud to have the Comet and it was used for a lot of VIP flights in those days. If anyone was visiting the country the RAF would go and pick them up. I did

A majestic image of RAF Comet C2 XK697 in flight. (BAE SYSTEMS)

one semi-VIP trip when we took some seriously important RAF officers and MPs on a tour of the Middle East. But that's the kind of thing the squadron did.

It was good for the air force that they could turn up all over the world. It was good more for Britain really, but the air force got a little of the kudos from it. You would turn up all over the world and this beautiful aircraft was sitting there with Royal Air Force Transport Command written all over it. I remember we were stuck at Travis Air Force Base north of San Francisco in January 1958 for five days because of the headwinds to Honolulu, there was nothing we could do about it but our aircraft was stuck outside the terminal building. It was a massive transport and bomber place and it had all sorts of super old four-engine, piston-driven aircraft all over the place and our beautiful sleek Comet was outside the building. About the third day they said could we come back and move it because they needed the space. It was on this area that was about the size of four football pitches and there was room for about another twenty Comets but no, we had to park the other side of the airfield. I knew why of course. They were fed up with all the beautiful remarks about it and not their own aircraft.

It used to be interesting flying over the States in the early days on my first tour because you'd call up, we didn't do airways because we were too high, we finished at 25,000 ft (7,620m) and started much higher but we'd get into American air space and you'd say 'RAF jet one two three, position such and such, at time such and such and 34,000 ft (10,363m) estimating such and such and 45 SOB as we used to say, souls on board,

Comet C2 XK716 taking off from Las Vegas McCarran in April 1959. (Private Collection)

and they'd say 'say again altitude', '34,000 ft climbing', 'Roger, roger, say again souls on board?', '45', 'roger that' and about five minutes later you'd have two jets, one either side looking at you. They never got used to it.

Every time we landed from an overseas flight we couldn't go home until we had been debriefed by de Havilland and Rolls-Royce and we told them everything. They would look at the logbook, quiz us on entries, discuss how things had happened and what we had done and what we had found and experienced. One of the flights they were interested in was the one where the autopilot failed after take-off from Lyneham and we hand-flew all the way to Adelaide and back. Although it was interesting, by God it was tiring. Of course, when we got back Rolls-Royce and de Havilland asked us everything and in fact they told us it was to help them make the next aircraft better, so of course we definitely helped the development of the Comet 4.

Brian had been a co-pilot for more than two years but he was not getting the flying hours to progress, so in 1959 he left the squadron, took a flying instructor's course at Little Rissington and trained cadets at Cranwell as a Qualified Flying Instructor

A line-up of both Comet C2s and C4s of 216 Squadron at RAF Lyneham. (Private Collection)

or QFI. By 1963, with plenty of hours in his logbook, Brian was offered the chance to return to 216 Squadron. By now the Comet C2s had been joined by the Comet C4.

*The Comet 4 was very much the king of the jungle but more to the point the Comet 2 had now been downgraded to a lower pressure difference, so everything was now done at 21 to 24,000 ft. The squadron was so much bigger, so much more impressive. There were virtually two squadrons, two flights if you like, and the numbers in the squadron had more-or-less doubled, Lyneham was much more buzzing, there was a new officers mess, a proper one, damn good food. The original officers mess was a Nissen hut close to the beginning of the runway, so it was a very noisy place when the Comets were taking off but very quiet when the Britannias were there.*

*The Comet 4 was the big boy but the Comet 2, although it was now downgraded in terms of pressurisation and therefore couldn't do the slip, was doing regular flights to Gibraltar, Luqa, Nicosia, or Akrotiri, Idris near Tripoli and the other one was El Adem but they were doing a lot of VIP stuff.*

*I got there in November, but I reached the squadron in January 1964 and did my training. By this time, instead of going to other places, the air force had got itself set properly and there was a Comet Air Training Squadron where I did all the ground school bits and pieces and then I could fly again. I went off on 2 February to Nicosia and did my conversion training, twenty-four hours flying in the right-hand seat.*

*I came back to the squadron and did my check flight in February 1964. After that I flew with any other captains who needed me and all of a sudden getting plenty of landings but because the Comet 4 was very busy with long range hauls down to Australia and to Hong Kong they didn't have that many of them to spare so we did the special VIP flights and lots of extra flights.*

*I joined the squadron in February and by May I was crewed up with a chap called Ron Underwood. Ron was a great captain. He looked after the co-pilot – me – and he was great to his crew. He had a wonderful attitude in that he cared, and was a true professional, but he was one of those blokes who cocked a snook at authority a bit. If he wanted to do something he would and Air Support Command headquarters, Transport as it was, were tremendous with their captains. They would stand by them all the time.*

*In about July, Ron became a VIP captain. Our first VIP trip was late October; Harold Wilson had just come to power again and Arthur Bottomley and his wife were going down to give independence to Northern Rhodesia to become Zambia. Southern Rhodesia, in the meantime, would become Rhodesia. We were positioned hurriedly in the morning to El Adem and we had to sleep during the day. The aircraft with him on board came from London that night and we went El Adem-Khartoum-Nairobi-Lusaka. We had to spend four hours on the ground in Nairobi because there was a meeting with Jomo Kenyatta. We tried to get some sleep for a couple of hours but that didn't work. We got down to Lusaka and, because it was a VIP flight we had to arrive on time.*

*Unfortunately, the navigator who set up the plan for us had allowed for half an hour too much, so we had to slow the aircraft right down to make sure we made the schedule at Lusaka which didn't help because by this time Ron and I kept falling asleep. The navigator was keeping us awake by hitting us with his ruler – navigator rulers were about two feet long – but anyway we took it in turns to sleep ten minutes on and ten minutes off. We were very tired, none of us had slept in El Adem and we had all been up for twenty-four hours now.*

We landed in Lusaka on time and the wing commander from the embassy came up to us and said 'Ah, I expect you chaps will want to get off to your accommodation. Unfortunately, the hotels are all full, but I've got you a big marquee in the grounds of the law school and it's separated so the ladies', because we had four female quartermasters with us, 'have got a special section'. The Captain said: 'We're not staying in a marquee! Where's the nearest hotel' and this chap said to Ron 'Salisbury' so Ron said 'OK, twenty tons of fuel please' and there we were knackered, but we got airborne and flew down to Salisbury and he said, 'as we've all been up this long let's all have a beer and get a good night's sleep'.

We decided to go to the swimming pool and a group captain came along. He said: 'Are you the RAF crew?' and Ron said 'Yes sir'. He said 'well you've got to leave the country, Ian Smith says you can't stay here', so we all turned up at RAF Salisbury and filed the flight plan to we didn't know where, and said we'd keep in touch.

We got airborne, went to Bulawayo and they didn't have any room for us, we went back towards Lusaka, but they still didn't have any room, we went to Livingstone and they said they had room for four people in the police station and four in the hotel and this was the day before independence. We took the rooms, the four officers stayed in the police station and the cabin crew stayed in the hotel.

Next morning, on the Saturday before independence, we all walked across to Southern Rhodesia and had our passports stamped Southern Rhodesia, we came back in and had our passports stamped Northern Rhodesia. The day after independence we went across to Victoria Falls and had our passports stamped Rhodesia, came back and had our passports stamped Zambia.

That night Arthur Bottomley said how proud he was to be in Gambia which I thought was a daft thing to do and, on the way back, we eventually left Livingstone and three

Prime Minister Harold Macmillan boards Comet C2 XK695 at London Airport on 7 May 1957. (BAE SYSTEMS)

*days later we went to Lusaka, picked him up, and off we went to El Adem via Nairobi and Khartoum, it was going to be a long night. We reached Nairobi and just as we got airborne we got a message from RAF Transport Command that we mustn't land in Khartoum. Fortunately, we had enough fuel, so we went across to Khormaksar in Aden and there was an RAF Comet 4 coming through just after we landed so our VIPs were transferred to that aircraft and we just went to the bar and had a few drinks before we went back the next day.*

In 1965 Brian was finally promoted to captain:

*If that had not been the future I wouldn't even have taken the job. I would have left. Like most pilots I only want to be in the left-hand seat.*

*So, Ron was posted to Belfasts and I wasn't a VIP co-pilot anymore. But on 15 October 1965, just after my twenty-ninth birthday, I flew my first flight as a captain. I did trips as a captain under training and flying solo as a captain without passengers and on 16 November I was a fully-fledged captain. My first ever proper trip was from Lyneham to Gibraltar and from then on, I only ever flew as captain.*

*It's a wonderful feeling of achievement, it's a great feeling of satisfaction. It's just what you aimed for, it's what you wanted and now you've got it.*

*I was a captain for just fifteen months before I went straight onto VC10s. I did my last two flights in the Comet 2 on 22 and 25 February 1967 the final flight of an aircraft to Benina and El Adem and the final flight to Luqa. I think there were two or three more in March and that was the finish of the Comet 2.*

*When the Comet 2 was finally finished, and the squadron received the VC10s, parked in a field at Brize Norton was a Comet 2 which was used for fire drills. It was a sad sight, as so many of us had been on the Comet 2 and we could look out of the window and watch this lovely Comet being desecrated, it was terrible. It was such a wicked place to put it. We loved the aeroplane.*

Peter Botwright signed on as early as 19 February 1946 and spent fifteen years flying fighters, first Meteors, then Vampires and Venoms in the Far East before joining a Javelin squadron in Germany. However a back injury meant that he could not use ejector seats and he returned to the UK for reallocation in 1963. He was to have the next part of his career on the Comet 4.

*Somebody, God bless them, said would you like to fly Comets, so I said, 'yes please'. Who wouldn't? But it was a long time coming because the RAF at that time didn't have a training school for Comet 4s. They only had five, so it wasn't worth it. I had to wait for a course to become available at Hatfield and then I had to wait for another course at Derby for the engines, so it was eight or nine months before I actually joined the squadron and started flying.*

Peter found that the Comet 4 had not lost the need for the famous gear change:

*When you throw the switch this thing motors along but in doing so it makes a slight pitch up and then pitch down and it finishes in exactly the same trim as before you started but you've got to remember that when the nose starts to come up you've got to push very gently forward* and then ease gently back for the other bit, it only takes a few seconds, and nobody else in the aircraft would even know you'd done it.

In my early days I was doing my first take-off and it was in the Far East and I was concentrating so much on getting the beacons right and all the other bits and pieces that Bob Hill, my captain, realised that I had forgotten about the gear change and he must have told me that he was doing it, but I didn't hear him and I was taken unawares when this thing pitched up and then pitched down. I was way behind the curve all the time.

One of the quartermasters down the back, a chap called Paddy O'Hare, was just about to leave the forward galley with a tray of orange juice for the passengers and one moment he was walking on tiptoe to stay in contact with the aeroplane and the next he was shrugged at the other end when it came up to meet him. He got rid of the orange juice and the first I knew was he came up and hit me over the head with the tray. It taught me a lesson and if Bob Hill had given me a jolly good telling off it wouldn't have made the same impression as Paddy did when he hit me with that tray, so I never forgot it again.

You came in as a junior co-pilot and you were cosseted a bit. You did a lot of flying in the Far East. I did Aden to Singapore about three

RAF Comet pilot Peter Botwright in 2017. (AFH)

Flying high above the airways, Comet C4 XR395 in November 1961. (BAE SYSTEMS)

*times, mainly because you didn't have to worry about navigation as you just headed off across the Indian Ocean. A bit more difficult to manage the navigation of it with a nav. aide because that was foreign to me. When I started on the Meteor we had two four-channel radios and that was it. If you'd just taken off from Wattisham and after twenty minutes someone said, 'what's your position', you'd say 'Suffolk', and, even then, you'd probably be wrong. We were just learning about jetstreams and if you found one suddenly you were half-way across the North Sea.*

*The controls were nicely balanced so there was nothing you had to worry about there and it was the sort of thing you could pick up very easily. You obviously can't fly it too fast or too slow, or bank too hard, but within the flight envelope it behaved just as you would expect it to.*

*Hatfield was having an open day and they wanted a Comet to come in. I thought, so did my boss, that it was just a fly-past, in which case anybody could do it and I got the job. But when I got there I was holding off, waiting for my time to come in, and the controller came on and said 'you're on, you've got four minutes'. I had no idea what I could do but the first thing I thought was to come over the hangars from behind so the crowd don't hear or see you, then open up because it makes quite a lot of noise, so that was the start of it and then I was turning it around with quite indecent amounts of bank and I did a slow fly-past with everything hanging down and hauled it round the corner. I was thoroughly enjoying myself and eventually the controller called up and said, 'are you enjoying yourself?' I said, 'yes I am' he said, 'so are we but unfortunately the next man is waiting to come in'.*

*That was an occasion when I could put more into the aeroplane than I could when it's full of passengers. We certainly exceeded 30 degrees of bank, that's for sure. Given the opportunity I wouldn't have minded trying a barrel roll in it.*

As already mentioned, right from the early days of the Comet 2, 216 Squadron was run like a scheduled airline. By this time it ran a 'slip' service entailing layovers along the route, as Peter recalls:

*An aeroplane left for Singapore every Wednesday and Sunday, and they did the rounds to Nicosia, Aden, round Egypt to Aden then it was Gan and on to Singapore. Then, after a while, we couldn't use Aden anymore, so we went through Bahrain.*

*You took the aeroplane from Lyneham to Bahrain and you'd offload, and you had a three or four day wait for the next aeroplane and you took that on to Singapore where you had another three or four days and you did the same thing on the way back.*

In 1965 the TSR2 project was cancelled. The following year Harold Wilson's government published a Defence Review. Some foreign governments accused Wilson of planning to abandon some of their NATO commitments and, in particular, many of those 'east of Suez'.

In January Wilson sent Defence Minister Denis Healey round the world to try to calm foreign nerves, and in particular those of major allies America and Australia. Healey's first stop was Washington to meet David Bruce, the US Ambassador to the UK, and George Ball, a State Department diplomat vehemently opposed to America's involvement in Vietnam. Peter Botwright tells the story of that journey:

*Left and below*: Two images of the various seating possibilities for the new RAF Comet C4. (BAE SYSTEMS)

*Well the longest trip I did was round the world with Healey. The range limits of the aeroplane were a bit constraining, so to get to Washington we couldn't fly straight across the Atlantic. We had to go down to Santa Maria in the Azores then across to Bermuda and up to Washington.*

*We were going into Andrews AFB at Washington and the weather forecast was appalling. It was a heavy snowstorm and I got the job of flying the aeroplane down the slope. I would get two commands from the captain, 'I have control' in which case I let go, 'overshoot' in which case I was to pull gently back and climb away. I didn't have to put the power on, or put the gear up, or the flaps or anything. The captain would do everything else for me.*

*The aeroplane is easy to fly so once it's set up it was on the glidepath all the way down. We went through 200 ft, and we went to 150 ft and 100 ft and nothing had happened, nobody had said anything and suddenly the captain said, 'I've got it', I let go and the next moment we hit the ground. I reverted to co-pilot and engaged reverse thrust and looked up. I couldn't see a thing for the snow. Reverse thrust didn't do much to help because it was throwing stuff up.*

*The controller then said, 'clear the runway quickly, you've got a C-130 up your arse' and then there was a jeep with two great red flashing lights to lead us off and the C-130 got in and then they closed the airfield. He just got in, like us, by the skin of his teeth and it was too bloody dangerous so they closed it.*

*When we landed we didn't realise we had ruined an engine so when we tried to take-off again to go to San Francisco one engine wouldn't spool up, so we had to taxy back, Healey and his men got on a civil aircraft to go on to Australia and we did a three-engine ferry to San Francisco. Lyneham flew out a new engine, a crew to change it and two crews in the Britannia and they made record time.*

*The Rolls-Royce man at San Francisco was very impressed. Then we went to Honolulu and a fairly long leg to Canton which is a little island in the middle of nowhere. It's only there because the US military had a tracking station for their satellites. I had the money, so I had to go and pay the landing fees and it's a civil airfield, not military and the chap didn't know, he said 'what is it?' I said, 'its a Comet' and he said, 'Hell, I don't know. Say five dollars'. From there it was Nandi and Canberra.*

The Comet caught up with Healey in Canberra where he was meeting with Australian Prime Minister, Robert Menzies:

*Coming back, it was Port Moresby, Labouan, Paya Lebar, Changi, Paya Lebar again and then back through Kuala Lumpur, Gan, Bahrain, Akrotiri and LAP. We were scheduled to go down to New Zealand, but Healey cancelled that bit.*

*We left on 25 January and we got back on 6 February. The biggest stop was San Francisco. We arrived on 28th and left on 31st.*

In March 1966 Peter was promoted to captain:

*Well it was strange really as I thought about the responsibility but so much of it was delegated that all you were doing was supervising to make sure everyone else had done their*

| | | | | | | |
|---|---|---|---|---|---|---|
| JANUARY | 25 | COMET 4C | 396 | S/L McCULLAGH | SELF | LYNEHAM - LAP |
| JANUARY | 26 | COMET 4C | 396 | S/L McCULLAGH | SELF | LAP - SANTA MARIA |
| JANUARY | 26 | COMET 4C | 396 | S/L McCULLAGH | SELF | SANTA MARIA - BERMUDA |
| JANUARY | 26 | COMET 4C | 396 | S/L McCULLAGH | SELF | BERMUDA - ANDREWS AFB |
| JANUARY | 28 | COMET 4C | 396 | S/L McCULLAGH | SELF | ANDREWS - SAN FRANCISCO |
| JANUARY | 31 | COMET 4C | 396 | S/L McCULLAGH | SELF | SAN FRANCISCO - HONOLULU |
| JANUARY | 31 | COMET 4C | 396 | S/L McCULLAGH | SELF | HONOLULU - CANTON |
| JANUARY | 31 | COMET 4C | 396 | S/L McCULLAGH | SELF | CANTON - NANDI |

*Above and below.* The pages from Peter Botwright's logbook showing the stages of his January-February 1966 round the world flight with Defence Minister Denis Healey. (Peter Botwright)

| | | | | | | |
|---|---|---|---|---|---|---|
| FEBRUARY | 1 | COMET 4C | 396 | S/L McCULLAGH | SELF | NANDI - CANBERRA |
| FEBRUARY | 2 | COMET 4C | 396 | S/L McCULLAGH | SELF | CANBERRA - PORT MORESBY |
| FEBRUARY | 2 | COMET 4C | 396 | S/L McCULLAGH | SELF | PORT MORESBY - LABUAN |
| FEBRUARY | 3 | COMET 4C | 396 | S/L McCULLAGH | SELF | LABUAN - PAYA LEBAR |
| FEBRUARY | 3 | COMET 4C | 396 | S/L McCULLAGH | SELF | PAYA LEBAR - CHANGI |
| FEBRUARY | 4 | COMET 4C | 396 | S/L McCULLAGH | SELF | CHANGI - PAYA LEBAR |
| FEBRUARY | 4 | COMET 4C | 396 | S/L McCULLAGH | SELF | PAYA LEBAR - KUALA LUMPUR |
| FEBRUARY | 5 | COMET 4C | 396 | S/L McCULLAGH | SELF | KL - GAN |
| FEBRUARY | 5 | COMET 4C | 396 | S/L McCULLAGH | SELF | GAN - BAHREIN |
| FEBRUARY | 6 | COMET 4C | 396 | S/L McCULLAGH | SELF | BAHREIN - AKROTIRI |
| FEBRUARY | 6 | COMET 4C | 396 | S/L McCULLAGH | SELF | AKROTIRI - LAP |
| FEBRUARY | 6 | COMET 4C | 396 | S/L McCULLAGH | SELF | LAP - LYNEHAM |
| FEBRUARY | 16 | COMET 4C | 398 | S/L BONNER | SELF | McT III |
| FEBRUARY | 18 | COMET 4C | 396 | F/L BUCKHAM | SELF | McT I + II |

job properly. Occasionally you have to make decisions, again that comes with experience. You can make the decision without too much head scratching and I never found it was much of a problem. I was thinking back to the days when I was first commissioned, and I had that little thin stripe on my arm and I felt the whole weight of the air force was on my shoulders and then fifteen years later there I am in command of a Comet and felt no weight of responsibility at all.

My first few trips were Lyneham-Nicosia-Bahrain-Gan-Changi and return to Lyneham, then Nicosia-Aden-Gan-Changi and return, and there were pages of that in the logbook before I got to go anywhere else. We were carrying troops and family and most of them were straight through to Singapore but there were the odd ones that were dropped off and ones that were picked up.

They made good use of the Comets, it was trooping up and down but there was the Britannia there as well. There were also civil aircraft doing it, but they had reduced in number somewhat. We always had a full aircraft. The only time the aircraft went out with any vacant space was if it was going to be a casevac and then you had to take some seats out and put some stretcher hangars in to bring people back.

We went out to Aden to pick up some troops. They'd driven their land rover over a missile I think and one of them had suffered quite a lot of chest injuries. He had to be brought back, unpressurised so that limited our height, and they also wanted as little turbulence as possible. This made it a bit of a trial for the navigator to work it out because we had to fly over the desert for a long way whichever way you go and that's usually a bit bumpy. So we took off at night and did the first bit of that and coming up through the Med we tried to fly off airways coming up Italy so we didn't get any of the turbulence from them. Then there were times we went to bring stretcher cases back from Changi, four or five of them.

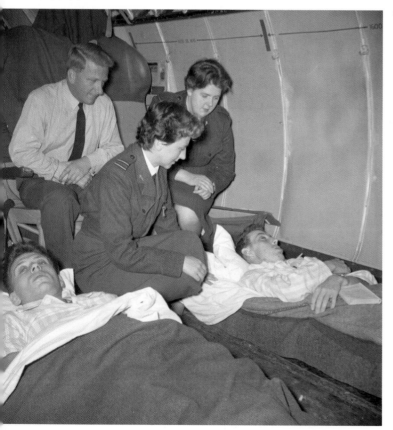

The Comet fleet took part in many casualty evacuations, bringing home injured and wounded servicemen from all round the globe. This is Comet C2 XK671 in 1957. (BAE SYSTEMS)

Peter stayed with 216 Squadron until 1968 when he left the RAF after twenty-two years of service. He continued flying for various other organisations until his retirement.

Between them Brian Burdett and Peter Botwright flew with the Comet 2s and Comet 4s of RAF Transport Command for more than twelve years. Perhaps Brian sums up the experience of the RAF Comet best:

At the time the Comet was wonderful because it had such a background, such a history, it was such an iconic aircraft that the sheer fact of being able to fly it was an honour and made you feel a special person.

Everywhere you went everyone wanted to see it, everyone wanted to look round it, crowd around it if they were allowed to and you got a sense that you were part of something important.

# The Comet Production List

| Construction No. | Series | Registration | Customer | First flight | Delivery | Subsequent Users |
|---|---|---|---|---|---|---|
| 6001 | 1 | G-5-1/G-ALVG | MoS | 27 Jul 49 | 1 Sep 49 | |
| 6002 | 1 | G-5-2/G-ALZK | MoS | 27 Jul 50 | 2 Apr 51 | |
| 6003 | 1 | G-ALYP | BOAC | 9 Jan 51 | 8 Apr 52 | |
| 6004 | 1 | G-ALYR | BOAC | 28 Jul 51 | 17 May 52 | |
| 6005 | 1 | G-ALYS | BOAC | 8 Sep 51 | 4 May 52 | |
| 6006 | 1 | G-ALYT/7610M | MoS | 16 Feb 52 | 1 Mar 52 | |
| 6007 | 1 | G-ALYU | BOAC | 13 Dec 51 | 6 Mar 52 | |
| 6008 | 1 | G-ALYV | BOAC | 9 Apr 52 | 23 Apr 52 | |
| 6009 | 1 | G-ALYW | BOAC | 25 May 52 | 14 Jun 52 | |
| 6010 | 1 | G-ALYX | BOAC | 9 Jul 52 | 25 Jul 52 | |
| 6011 | 1 | G-ALYY | BOAC | 10 Sep 52 | 23 Sep 52 | |
| 6012 | 1 | G-ALYZ | BOAC | 23 Sep 52 | 30 Sep 52 | |
| 6013 | 1A | CF-CUM/G-ANAV | (CP) BOAC | 11 Aug 52 | 12 Aug 53 | |
| 6014 | 1A | CF-CUN | CP | 24 Dec 52 | 2 Mar 52 | |
| 6015 | 1A | F-BGSA | UAT | 13 Nov 52 | 11 Dec 52 | |
| 6016 | 1A | F-BGSB | UAT | 21 Jan 53 | 19 Feb 53 | |
| 6017 | 1A | VC5301 | RCAF | 21 Feb 53 | 18 Mar 53 | |
| 6018 | 1A | VC5302/CF-SVR/N373S | RCAF | 25 Mar 53 | 13 Apr 53 | RCR; BL |
| 6019 | 1A | F-BGSC | UAT | 15 Apr 53 | 30 Apr 53 | |
| 6020 | 1A | F-BGNX/G-AOJT | AF | 13 Nov 52 | 11 Dec 52 | MoS |
| 6021 | 1A | F-BGNY/G-AOJU/XM829 | AF | 22 May 53 | 7 Jul 53 | DH; A&AEE |
| 6022 | 1A | F-BGNZ/XM823/G-APAS/8351M | AF | 16 Mar 53 | 22 Jul 53 | RAF |
| 6023 | 2R | (G-AMXA)/XK655 | (MoS) RAF | 29 Aug 53 | 17 Feb 56 | |
| 6024 | 2T | (G-AMXB)/XK669 | (MoS) RAF | 3 Nov 53 | 8 Jun 56 | |
| 6025 | 2R | (G-AMXC)/XK659 | (MoS) RAF | 25 Nov 53 | 12 Jul 57 | |
| 6026 | 2E | (G-AMXD)/XN453 | (MoS) RAF | 20 Aug 54 | 29 Aug 57 | |

| Construction No. | Series | Registration | Customer | First flight | Delivery | Subsequent Users |
|---|---|---|---|---|---|---|
| 6027 | 2R | (G-AMXE)/XK663 | (MoS) RAF | 18 Jul 55 | 19 Apr 57 | |
| 6028 | T2 | (G-AMXF)/XK670/7926M | (MoS) RAF | 12 Mar 56 | 7 Jun 56 | |
| 6029 | C2 | (G-AMXG)/XK671/7927M | (MoS) RAF | 16 Jul 56 | 22 Aug 56 | |
| 6030 | C2 | (G-AMXH)/XK695/9164M | RAF | 21 Aug 56 | 14 Sep 56 | |
| 6031 | C2 | (G-AMXI)/XK696 | RAF | 29 Sep 56 | 14 Nov 56 | |
| 6032 | C2 | (G-AMXJ)/XK697 | RAF | 17 Nov 56 | 12 Dec 56 | |
| 6033 | 2E | (G-AMXK)/XV144 | MoS | 10 Jul 57 | 26 Aug 57 | RAE |
| 6034 | C2 | (G-AMXL)/XK698/8031M | RAF | 13 Dec 56 | 9 Jan 57 | |
| 6035 | C2 | XK699/7971M | RAF | 2 Feb 57 | 20 Feb 57 | |
| 6036 | 2 | Test airframe | MoS | | | |
| 6037 | C2 | XK715/7905M | RAF | 26 Apr 57 | 22 May 57 | |
| 6038 | Not completed | | | | | |
| 6039 | Not built | | | | | |
| 6040 | Not built | | | | | |
| 6041 | Not built | | | | | |
| 6042 | Not built | | | | | |
| 6043 | Not built | | | | | |
| 6044 | Not built | | | | | |
| 6045 | C2 | XK716/7958M | RAF | 6 May 57 | 7 May 57 | |
| 6100 | 3 | G-ANLO/XP915 | MoA | 19 July 54 | RAF; RAE | |
| 6401 | 4 | G-APDA/9M-AOA/9V-BAS | BOAC | 27 Apr 58 | 24 Feb 59 | AC; MSA; DAL(s) |
| 6402 | 4 | Test airframe | | | | |
| 6403 | 4 | G-APDB/9M-AOB | BOAC 27 Jul 58 | 30 Sep 58 | MSA; DAL; DAS | |
| 6404 | 4 | G-APDC/9M-AOC/9V-BAT | BOAC 23 Sep 58 | 30 Sep 58 | MSA; DAL | |
| 6405 | 4 | G-APDD/9M-AOD/5Y-AMT | BOAC | 5 Nov 58 | 18 Nov 58 | MSA; EA; DAL |
| 6406 | 4 | G-APDE/9M-AOE/9V-BAU/5Y-ALF | BOAC | 20 Sep 58 | 2 Oct 58 | MSA; EA; DAL |
| 6407 | 4 | G-APDF/XV814 | BOAC | 11 Dec 58 | 31 Dec 58 | AC; MoS |
| 6408 | 4 | LV-PLM/LV-AHN | AA | 11 Dec 58 | 2 Mar 59 | DAL(s) |
| 6409 | 4 | G-APDH | BOAC | 21 Nov 58 | 6 Dec 58 | MSA |

| Construction No. | Series | Registration | Customer | First flight | Delivery | Subsequent Users |
|---|---|---|---|---|---|---|
| 6410 | 4 | LV-PLO/LV-AHO | AA | 25 Feb 59 | 18 Mar 59 | |
| 6411 | 4 | LV-PLP/LV-AHP | AA | 24 Mar 59 | 2 May 59 | |
| 6412 | 4 | G-APDK/5Y-ALD | BOAC | 2 Jan 59 | 12 Feb 59 | EA; DAL |
| 6413 | 4 | G-APDL/5Y-ADD | BOAC | 27 Apr 59 | 6 May 59 | EA; QM |
| 6414 | 4 | G-APDM/OD-AEV/9V-BBJ | BOAC | 21 Mar 59 | 16 Apr 59 | QA; MEA; MSA; DAL |
| 6415 | 4 | G-APDN | BOAC | 29 May 59 | 19 Jun 59 | AC; MA; KU; DAL |
| 6416 | 4 | G-APDO | BOAC | 29 Apr 59 | 14 May 59 | DAL |
| 6417 | 4 | G-APDP/9V-BBH/XX944 | BOAC | 29 May 59 | 11 Jun 59 | QA; AC; MSA; DAL |
| 6418 | 4 | G-APDR/XA-NAZ/XA-NAP | BOAC | 9 Jul 59 | 20 Jul 59 | AI (charter); MX; CAW |
| 6419 | 4 | G-APDS | BOAC | 6 Aug 59 | 16 Aug 59 | AC (charter); KU |
| 6420 | 4 | G-APDT/XA-POW/XA-NAB | BOAC | 2 Oct 59 | 19 Oct 59 | MX; BA |
| 6421 | 4B | G-APMA | BEA | 27 Jun 59 | 20 Dec 59 | |
| 6422 | 4B | G-APMB | BEA | 17 Aug 59 | 9 Nov 59 | CA; DAL; BAA |
| 6423 | 4B | G-APMC | BEA | 1 Oct 59 | 16 Nov 59 | BEAA; DAL(s) |
| 6424 | 4C | XA-NAR | MX | 31 Oct 59 | 8 Jun 60 | GU |
| 6425 | 4C | XA-NAS/N99WA | MX | 3 Dec 59 | | WA; RA |
| 6426 | 4B | G-APMF | BEA | 5 Jan 60 | 27 Jan 60 | BEAA; DAL |
| 6427 | 4 | G-APDG/9K-ACI | BOAC | 12 Nov 59 | 28 Nov 59 | KU; DAL |
| 6428 | 4 | G-APDI/HC-ALT | BOAC | 7 Dec 59 | 18 Dec 59 | MA; AE |
| 6429 | 4 | G-APDJ | BOAC | 23 Dec 59 | 11 Jan 60 | AC; DAL |
| 6430 | 4 | LV-POY/LV-AHR | AA | 15 Feb 60 | 8 Mar 60 | |
| 6431 | 4 | VP-KPJ/5X-AAO | EAA | 14 Jul 60 | 25 Jul 60 | DAL (s) |
| 6432 | 4 | LV-POZ/LV-AHS/G-AZLW | AA | 18 Feb 60 | 19 Mar 60 | DAL |
| 6433 | 4 | VP-KPK/5H-AAF | EAA | 28 Jul 60 | 6 Sep 60 | DAL (s) |
| 6434 | 4 | LV-PPA/LV-AHU/G-AZIY | AA | 2 Jul 60 | 26 Jul 60 | DAL |
| 6435 | 4B | G-APMD | BEA | 17 Mar 60 | 29 Mar 60 | BEAA; DAL |
| 6436 | 4B | G-APME | BEA | 26 Apr 60 | 10 May 60 | DAL |
| 6437 | 4B | G-APYC/SX-DAK | BEA/OA | 7 Apr 60 | 26 Apr 60 | DAL |
| 6438 | 4B | G-APYD/SX-DAL | BEA/OA | 3 May 60 | 14 May 60 | CA; DAL |
| 6439 | 4C | SU-ALC | MI/UAA | 21 May 60 | 10 Jun 60 | |
| 6440 | 4B | G-APZM/SX-DAN | BEA/OA | 30 Jun 60 | 14 Jul 60 | CA; DAL |

| Construction No. | Series | Registration | Customer | First flight | Delivery | Subsequent Users |
|---|---|---|---|---|---|---|
| 6441 | 4C | SU-ALD | MI/UAA | 15 Jun 60 | 26 Jun 60 | |
| 6442 | 4B | G-APMG | BEA | 25 Jul 60 | 31 Jul 60 | BEAA; DAL |
| 6443 | 4C | XA-NAT/N777WA | MX | 7 Oct 60 | 29 Nov 60 | GU; RA |
| 6444 | 4C | SU-ALE | UAA | 22 Nov 60 | 23 Dec 60 | |
| 6445 | 4C | OD-ADR | MEA | 3 Dec 60 | 19 Dec 60 | |
| 6446 | 4C | OD-ADQ | MEA | 4 Feb 61 | 15 Feb 61 | |
| 6447 | 4B | G-ARDI | | 18 Mar 61 | 25 Mar 61 | CA; DAL(s) |
| 6448 | 4C | OD-ADS | MEA | 5 Mar 61 | 14 Mar 61 | |
| 6449 | 4B | G-ARCO | BEA | 5 Apr 61 | 13 Apr 61 | |
| 6450 | 4C | OD-ADT | MEA | 9 Mar 61 | 18 Mar 61 | DAL |
| 6451 | 4B | G-ARCP/G-BBUV | BEA | 11 Apr 61 | 19 Apr 61 | BEAA; DAL |
| 6452 | 4B | G-ARJK | BEA/OA | 4 May 61 | 15 May 61 | BEAA; DAL |
| 6453 | 4B | G-ARGM | BEA | 27 Apr 61 | 6 May 61 | BEAA; DAL(s) |
| 6454 | 4C | SU-ALL | UAA | 30 May 61 | 12 Jun 61 | DAL |
| 6455 | 4B | G-ARJL | BEA/OA | 19 May 61 | 31 May 61 | BEAA; DAL(s) |
| 6456 | 4B | G-ARJM | BEA | 8 Jun 61 | 26 Jun 61 | |
| 6457 | 4C | ST-AAW/G-ASDZ | SA | 5 Nov 61 | 14 Nov 62 | DAL(s) |
| 6458 | 4C | SU-ALM/G-BEEX | UAA | 30 Jun 61 | 15 Jul 61 | EA; DAL(s) |
| 6459 | 4B | G-ARJN | BEA | 21 Jul 61 | 4 Aug 61 | BEAA; DAL |
| 6460 | 4C | LV-PTS/ G-AROV/ LV-AIB | AA | 21 Aug 61 | 27 Apr 62 | DAL |
| 6461 | 4C | SA-R-7 | GSA | 29 Mar 62 | | |
| 6462 | 4C | SU-AMV/G-BEEY | UAA | 25 Mar 62 | 6 Apr 62 | EA; DAL(s) |
| 6463 | 4C | ST-AAX/ G-BDIF | SA | 8 Dec 62 | 21 Dec 62 | DAL |
| 6464 | 4C | SU-AMW | UAA | 3 Apr 62 | 16 Apr 62 | |
| 6465 | 4C | 9K-ACA/G-AYWX | KA | 14 Dec 62 | 18 Jan 63 | MEA; DAL |
| 6466 | 4C | SU-ANC/G-BEEZ | UAA | 8 Dec 62 | 22 Dec 62 | EA; DAL(s) |
| 6467 | C4 | XR395/G-BDIT | RAF | 15 Nov 61 | 1 Jun 62 | DAL |
| 6468 | C4 | XR396/G-BDIU | RAF | 28 Dec 61 | 12 Mar 62 | DAL |
| 6469 | C4 | XR397/G-BDIV | RAF | 17 Jan 62 | 15 Feb 62 | DAL |
| 6470 | C4 | XR398/G-BDIW | RAF | 13 Feb 62 | 13 Mar 62 | DAL |
| 6471 | C4 | XR399/G-BDIX | RAF | 20 Mar 62 | 26 Apr 62 | DAL |
| 6472 | 4C | VP-KRL/5Y-AAA | EAA | 12 Mar 62 | 10 Apr 62 | DAL(s) |
| 6473 | 4C | XS235/G-CPDA | A&AEE | 26 Sep 63 | 21 Dec 63 | CW |
| 6474 | 4C | 9K-ACE/G-AYVS | KU | 17 Dec 63 | 2 Feb 64 | MEA; DAL |
| 6475 | 4C | SU-ANI | UAA | 4 Feb 64 | 26 Feb 64 | |

# KEY

| | |
|---|---|
| A&AEE | Aeroplane and Armament Experimental Establishment |
| AA | Aerolineas Argentinas |
| AC | Air Ceylon |
| AE | AREA Ecuador |
| AF | Air France |
| AI | Air India |
| BA | British Airways |
| BAA | British Airports Authority |
| BEA | British European Airways |
| BEAA | BEA Airtours |
| BL | Bellomy Lawson |
| BOAC | British Overseas Airways Corporation |
| CA | Channel Airways |
| CP | Canadian Pacific |
| CW | C. Walton Ltd |
| DAL | Dan-Air London |
| DAS | Duxford Aviation Society |
| DH | De Havilland |
| EA | Egyptair |
| EAA | East African Airways |
| GSA | Government of Saudi Arabia |
| GU | Guest Mexicana |
| KU | Kuwait |
| MA | Malaysian Airline System |
| MEA | Middle East Airlines |
| MI | Misrair |
| MoA | Ministry of Aviation |
| MoS | Ministry of Supply |
| MSA | Malaysia-Singapore Airlines |
| MX | Mexicana |
| OA | Olympic Airways |
| QA | Qantas |
| QM | Qantas          Malaysian |
| RA | Redmond Air |
| RAE | Royal Aircraft Establishment |
| RAF | Royal Air Force |
| RCAF | Royal Canadian Air Force |
| RCR | R.C. Rose |
| (s) | Used as spares |
| SA | Sudan Airways |
| UAA | United Arab Airways |
| UAT | Union Aéromaritime de Transport |
| WA | Westernair |

# List of Comet Survivors

| | | |
|---|---|---|
| Comet 1A | G-APAS | RAF Museum, Cosford |
| Comet 1A | F-BGNX | De Havilland Museum, London Colney (fuselage only) |
| | 5301 | Canada Aviation and Space Museum, Ottawa |
| Comet 2R | XK695 | De Havilland Museum, London Colney (nose only) |
| Comet C2 | XK699 | Boscombe Down Collection, Old Sarum (remains) |
| Comet C2/R2 | G-AMXA | Al Mahatta Museum, Sharjah (nose only) |
| Comet 4 | G-APDB | Imperial War Museum Duxford |
| Comet 4 | G-APDF | Chipping Camden, Gloucestershire (privately-held; nose only) |
| Comet 4B | G-APYD | Science Museum, Wroughton |
| Comet 4C | G-BDIX | National Museum of Flight, East Fortune |
| Comet 4C | G-BDIW | Flugausstellung Hermeskeil, Germany |
| Comet 4C | G-CPDA | Bruntingthorpe, Leicestershire |
| Comet 4C | N888WA | Museum of Flight, Seattle, USA |
| Comet 4C | G-BEEX | North East Aircraft Museum, Tyne and Wear (nose only) |
| Comet 4C | N777WA | Parque Zoologico Irapuato, Mexico |

The de Havilland Museum at London Colney also displays an original Comet 4 flight simulator used for crew training. Supplied to BOAC it was transferred to Dan-Air in 1970. It was stored at the Science Museum's Wroughton facility before being offered to the de Havilland Museum in 1996.